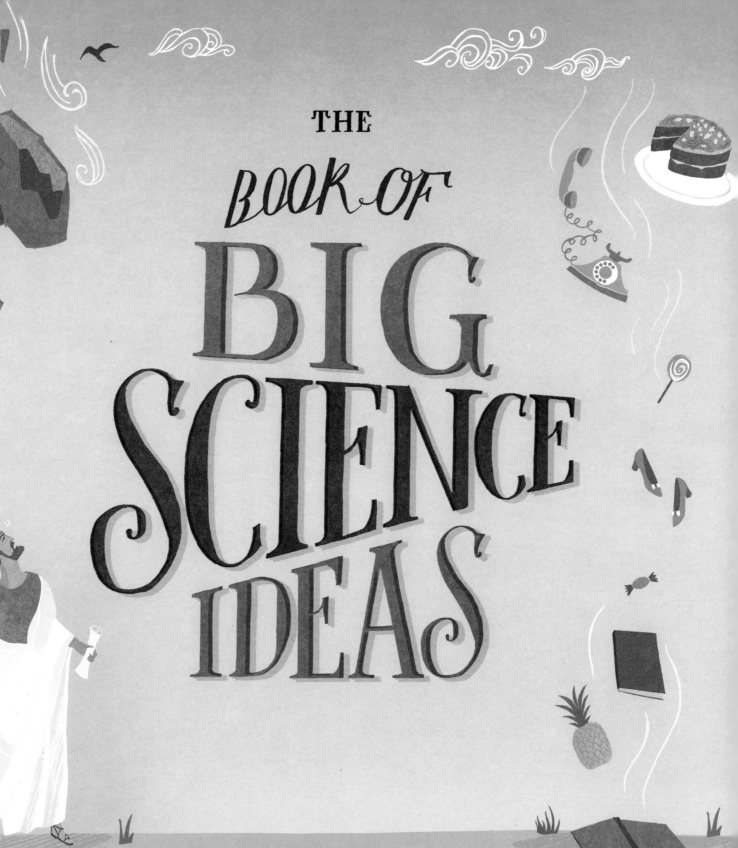

THE
BOOK OF
BIG
SCIENCE
IDEAS

FREYA HARDY

Illustrated by
SARA MULVANNY

IVY KIDS

First published in the UK in 2019 by

Ivy Kids

An imprint of The Quarto Group
The Old Brewery
6 Blundell Street
London N7 9BH
United Kingdom
www.QuartoKnows.com

British Library Cataloguing-in-Publication Data
A catalogue record for this book is available from the British Library.

ISBN: 978-1-78240-738-6

This book was conceived, designed & produced by

Ivy Kids

58 West Street, Brighton BN1 2RA, United Kingdom

PUBLISHER Susan Kelly
MANAGING EDITOR Susie Behar
ART DIRECTOR Hanri van Wyk
DESIGNER Claire Munday
IN-HOUSE DESIGNER Kate Haynes
PROJECT EDITOR Hannah Dove
ASSISTANT EDITOR Lucy Menzies
CONSULTANT Dr Sarah Bearchell
FACT CHECKER Tom Jackson

Manufactured in Guangdong, China TT072019

1 3 5 7 9 10 8 6 4 2

Contents

WHY DO IDEAS MATTER? · 4-5

THE SCIENTIFIC METHOD · 6-7

BIG idea 1 EVERYTHING IS MADE OF ATOMS · 8-11

BIG idea 2 ELEMENTS CAN BE ORDERED · 12-15

BIG idea 3 EVERYTHING REVOLVES AROUND THE SUN · 16-19

BIG idea 4 WHAT GOES UP... MUST COME DOWN! · 20-23

BIG idea 5 THE UNIVERSE IS EXPANDING · 24-27

BIG idea 6 LIFE CAN BE ORDERED · 28-31

BIG idea 7 SPECIES CHANGE OVER TIME · 32-35

BIG idea 8 BACTERIA CAUSE INFECTIOUS DISEASE · 36-39

BIG idea 9 IT'S ALL IN THE GENES · 40-43

BIG idea 10 ENERGY CANNOT BE CREATED OR DESTROYED · 44-47

BIG idea 11 CHARGED PARTICLES CREATE ELECTRICITY · 48-51

BIG idea 12 FOSSIL FUELS WILL RUN OUT · 52-55

BIG idea 13 MACHINES CAN SOLVE PROBLEMS · 56-59

BIG idea 14 INFORMATION IS VALUABLE · 60-63

BIG idea 15 MACHINES CAN LEARN · 64-67

FUTURE BIG IDEAS · 68-69

MORE BIG THINKERS YOU SHOULD KNOW ABOUT · 70-71

TIMELINE OF BIG SCIENCE IDEAS · 72-75

GLOSSARY · 76-80

Why do ideas matter?

IDEAS – EVEN SILLY ONES – ARE MIGHTY POWERFUL. THEY'RE IMPORTANT. THEY CHANGE THINGS.

A single idea can start a war, save or take billions of lives, rearrange the universe, or simply make a person giggle until they wee a little bit. Ideas can be widely believed but spectacularly wrong, or undoubtedly right and totally ignored!

This book looks at 15 big science ideas. Each one has two spreads: the first explains the idea and the second looks at some of the ingenious thinkers who helped to shape it. Tricky words are highlighted in bold and can be looked up in the glossary.

Each idea and thinker in this book can teach us a lot. Not just about science, but about the importance of determination and the value of being curious and interested in the world.

Take a look at the opposite page for a sneak peek at some of the lessons you'll learn!

10 THINGS YOU WILL LEARN FROM THIS BOOK:

1. No matter how clever you are or how amazing you think your idea is, everyone can make mistakes. You can always learn new things.

2. It's possible for two people to have the same idea at once.

3. An idea can look and feel right and, even if it's better than other ideas around at that moment, it can still be proven false.

4. Sometimes it's important to stand up for your ideas, even if other people don't like them at all.

5. Often, great ideas go unrecognized for long periods of time, but history usually gives the credit to the right people in the end.

6. Sometimes you need to experiment and get your hands dirty to prove your hypothesis.

7. It's possible to have the right idea and still come to the wrong conclusions.

8. It's good to remember that most big ideas are the result of work by many different thinkers.

9. You don't have to be a scientist to have big science ideas.

10. Some ideas can only be described as bonkers.

Nicolaus Copernicus knew his idea could put his life at risk, but he published it all the same, even if he did wait until he was on his death bed! (See Big Idea 3.)

Charles Darwin and Alfred Russel Wallace both thought up the idea of evolution (see Big Idea 7).

Friedrich Miescher (see Big Idea 9) inspected pus-soaked bandages to find out more about human biology. That can't have been pretty!

Rosalind Franklin's work on DNA was forgotten for a while, but today we remember her impact (see Big Idea 9).

Dmitri Mendeleev (see Big Idea 2) created the periodic table, but it has taken many more chemists after him, like Marie Curie, to keep it up to date.

Mary Anning (Big Idea 7), Ada Lovelace (Big Idea 13) and Isaac Asimov (Big Idea 15) weren't scientists, but their work led to major scientific discoveries.

Anaximander, with his idea of fishy humans (see Big Idea 7), and Benjamin Franklin, with his plan to fly a kite into a thunderstorm (see Big Idea 11) both had some eccentric ideas.

5

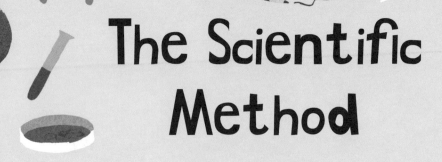

The Scientific Method

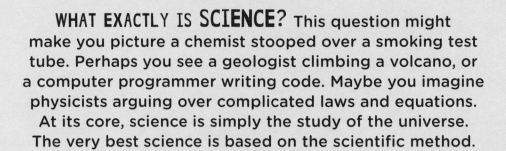

WHAT EXACTLY IS SCIENCE? This question might make you picture a chemist stooped over a smoking test tube. Perhaps you see a geologist climbing a volcano, or a computer programmer writing code. Maybe you imagine physicists arguing over complicated laws and equations. At its core, science is simply the study of the universe. The very best science is based on the scientific method.

WHAT IS THE SCIENTIFIC METHOD?

The scientific method is a step-by-step process used by scientists to investigate ideas. Scientists can use the method no matter what they're investigating — which is handy! But the best thing about the method is that it makes sure any findings (or answers) are based on evidence (measurable proof). And evidence is KEY to good science.

The basic method is:

1. Research — make observations

2. Question — ask questions about your research

3. Hypothesis — come up with theories or predictions about your research

4. Experiment — test your theories

5. Analysis — study the evidence gathered from your experiment

6. Conclusion — present and discuss your results.

We haven't ALWAYS used the scientific method. In fact, lots of the big thinkers in this book based their conclusions on thoughts, feelings and some pretty shoddy experiments. But don't look back too harshly: each strange idea or ill-researched theory has shaped our understanding and helped science evolve. In science, it's OK to be proved wrong! If we had all the answers, then there'd be no NEW big ideas! And who wants that?

READY, SET, EXPERIMENT!

Here's an example of how to use the scientific method...

RESEARCH

It's a hot summer's day and you're drinking a glass of cold water with a big fat ice cube in it. You notice the ice cube is melting.

QUESTION

As you observe it melting, you wonder, 'Will ice cubes melt just as fast in other liquids too?'

HYPOTHESIS

This leads you to make a prediction: 'I think ice cubes melt faster in water than in other cold liquids'.

EXPERIMENT

You decide to test your theory. You experiment by dropping an ice cube into a glass of water and timing how long it takes to melt. You then repeat the test: first you use milk, then you use orange juice (no bits!) and finally you use lemonade.

Each time, the glass, the size of the ice cube, and the temperature and amount of liquid stay the same — we call these the 'control variables'. The melting ice cube is what you are observing — we call this the 'dependent variable'. The liquid is the only thing you change each time — we call this the 'independent variable'.

ANALYSIS

When each ice cube has melted and you've recorded the timings (and drunk four glasses of ice-cold liquid), you can begin to study your findings.

CONCLUSION

At last, you can shout it from the roof tops — you have the answer! (No spoilers here, you'll have to test it yourself!)

Everything is made of atoms

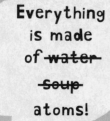

Everything is made of ~~water~~ ~~soup~~ atoms!

WHAT IS EVERYTHING MADE OF? This riddle has been puzzling us for centuries. For some, the answer was water. Others thought we evolved from a weird kind of space soup. Today, we know that atoms are the building blocks of everything. This book, you, ice cream — it's all made of atoms.

WHAT EXACTLY IS AN ATOM?

The big idea that everything is made of atoms is called **atomic theory**. The word 'atom' comes from the Greek word *atomos*, meaning 'indivisible'. The name was a good one, because we used to think atoms were the smallest **particles** in existence. They are very small — this dot '.' is about 10 million times the size of an atom — but in fact, they are made of three tinier particles, called **protons**, **neutrons** and **electrons**.

ARE ALL ATOMS THE SAME?

There are different kinds of atoms, based on the number of protons, neutrons and electrons they contain, and how these particles are organized. Each kind of atom makes up an **element** (a pure substance made from a single type of atom). Oxygen, hydrogen, helium and carbon are all elements.

When atoms combine with other atoms they form **molecules**. It takes a lot of atoms to make up enough molecules to form any thing. There are almost 7 billion, billion, billion atoms in an average human!

When you think of Earth's 7 billion humans and everything else in the universe — well, that's a mindboggling number of atoms.

Elements in the human body:

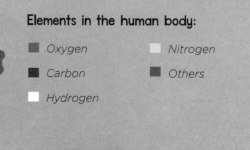

- Oxygen
- Nitrogen
- Carbon
- Others
- Hydrogen

THE **STRUCTURE** OF ATOMS

At the atom's centre is the **nucleus**, containing protons and neutrons.
Around it are energy levels — each level holds a certain number of
electrons. Here is the structure of a carbon atom:

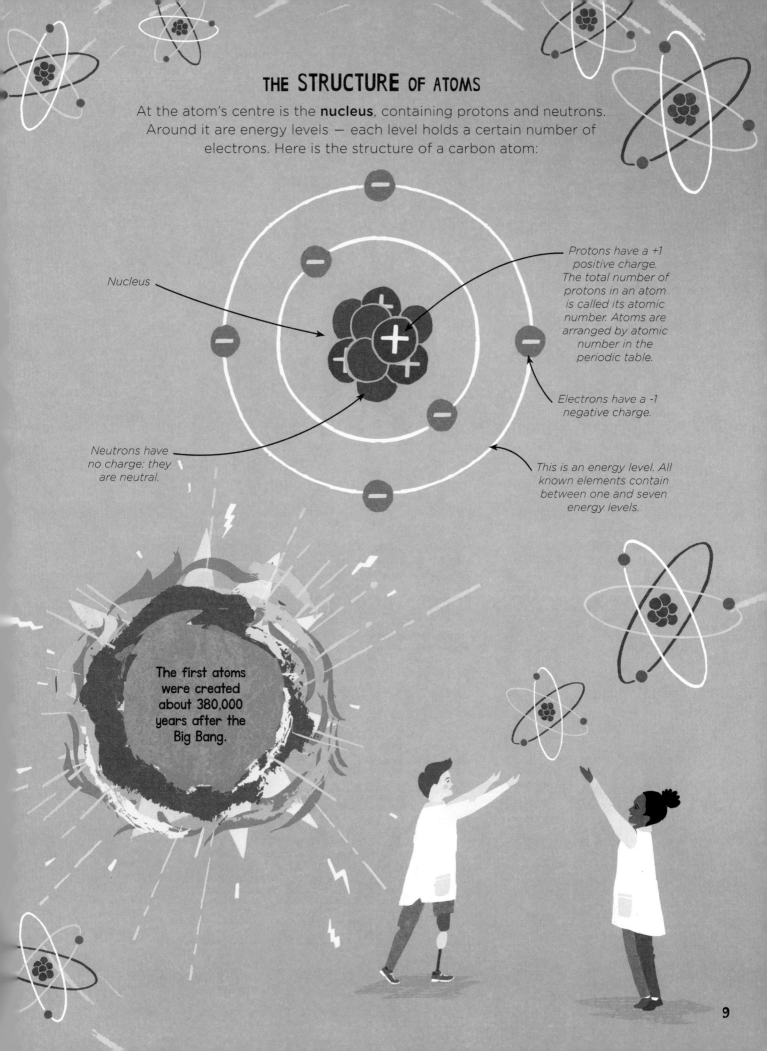

Nucleus

Protons have a +1
positive charge.
The total number of
protons in an atom
is called its atomic
number. Atoms are
arranged by atomic
number in the
periodic table.

Electrons have a -1
negative charge.

Neutrons have
no charge: they
are neutral.

This is an energy level. All
known elements contain
between one and seven
energy levels.

The first atoms
were created
about 380,000
years after the
Big Bang.

The Big Thinkers

Now we know about atoms, let's explore how this Big Idea began, then grew. Over the centuries, lots of people contributed to our understanding of atoms. Here are four of the thinkers who helped shape atomic theory.

DEMOCRITUS
c. 460-370 BCE

The Ancient Greek Democritus was one of the first to suggest that all matter is made of indivisible particles called *atomos*. He proposed that atoms had their own weight, size and shape. He also thought that atoms had similar qualities to the substances they made, so iron atoms would be iron-y, clay atoms squidgy and jam particles would be... yummy!

His rival, Aristotle, disagreed. He thought that everything was made of earth, water, air and fire. People believed Aristotle, and the idea of atoms was ignored for about 2,000 years.

The one who thought it!

The one who proved it!

JOHN DALTON
1766-1844

John Dalton was an English chemist whose family was so poor he was forced to leave formal education aged 10. Despite this, he went on to lay the foundations for what we know about atoms today.

Dalton's atomic theory proposed that:

• All elements are made of atoms.

• The atoms of one element are identical, and unique to that element.

• Atoms cannot be divided, created or destroyed.

• Atoms of different elements bond together in specific combinations to form chemical **compounds**.

Erm... excuse me

Irish chemist William Higgins claimed to have discovered atomic theory before Dalton. It's definitely possible that Higgins' book on the subject influenced his rival.

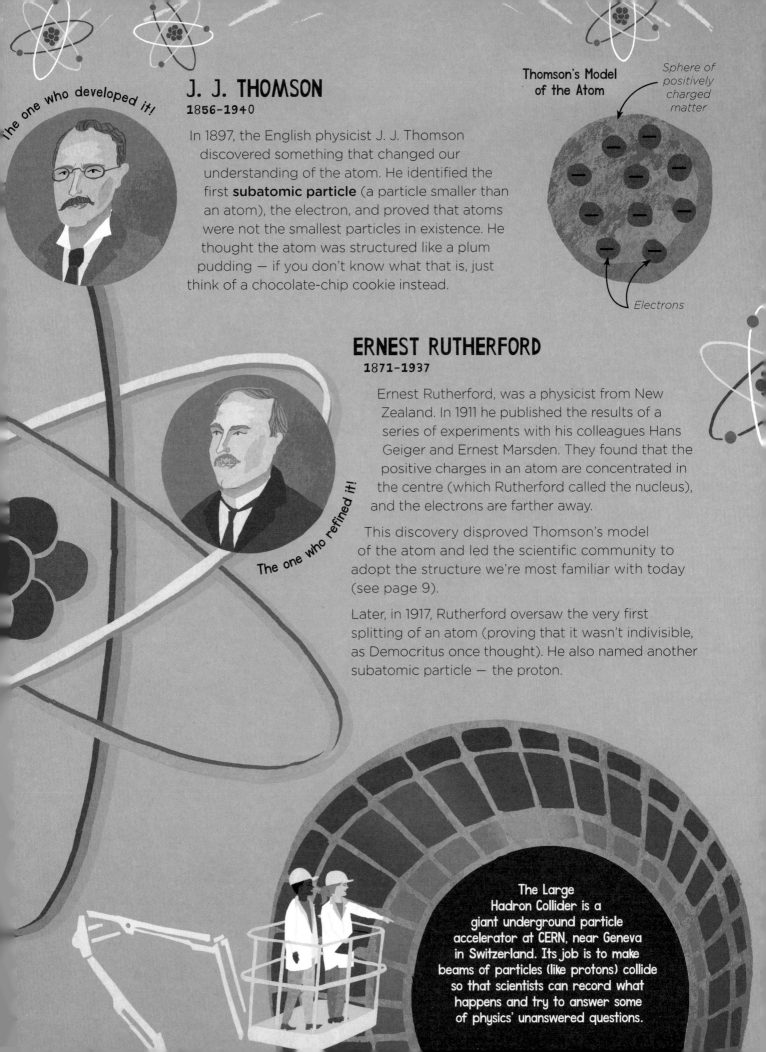

J. J. THOMSON
1856-1940

In 1897, the English physicist J. J. Thomson discovered something that changed our understanding of the atom. He identified the first **subatomic particle** (a particle smaller than an atom), the electron, and proved that atoms were not the smallest particles in existence. He thought the atom was structured like a plum pudding — if you don't know what that is, just think of a chocolate-chip cookie instead.

Thomson's Model of the Atom

Sphere of positively charged matter

Electrons

ERNEST RUTHERFORD
1871-1937

Ernest Rutherford, was a physicist from New Zealand. In 1911 he published the results of a series of experiments with his colleagues Hans Geiger and Ernest Marsden. They found that the positive charges in an atom are concentrated in the centre (which Rutherford called the nucleus), and the electrons are farther away.

This discovery disproved Thomson's model of the atom and led the scientific community to adopt the structure we're most familiar with today (see page 9).

Later, in 1917, Rutherford oversaw the very first splitting of an atom (proving that it wasn't indivisible, as Democritus once thought). He also named another subatomic particle — the proton.

The Large Hadron Collider is a giant underground particle accelerator at CERN, near Geneva in Switzerland. Its job is to make beams of particles (like protons) collide so that scientists can record what happens and try to answer some of physics' unanswered questions.

Elements can be ordered

HOW DO WE MAKE SENSE OF ALL THE STUFF IN THE UNIVERSE?
The universe is full of elements — simple substances that cannot be broken down into simpler ones. We recognize 118 elements today, but the list is growing. To study, compare and find new elements, scientists use the periodic table.

WHAT IS THE PERIODIC TABLE?

It's a table of all the known chemical elements in existence. Each period (or row) is arranged by increasing **atomic number** (the total number of protons in the atom's nucleus) and follows a pattern of **properties**. A new row begins each time the pattern repeats. This means that each group (or column) contains elements with similar characteristics and behaviours. Handy!

Elements are particular types of atom. See Big Idea 1.

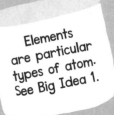

WHAT'S SO GREAT ABOUT THE PERIODIC TABLE?

At first, the periodic table was used to help discover more elements. It worked like a jigsaw puzzle. Suppose scientists knew about silicon and tin, but needed to know what came between them. They could use the patterns in the periodic table to find out the missing element's atomic number, what it might look like and how it might behave. Step forward germanium! They wouldn't even have to go out and find it — that could happen later on.

Today, scientists still try to discover new elements, but it doesn't happen as often anymore. We mostly use the periodic table to quickly see which elements share characteristics and to predict how they will behave.

THE PERIODIC TABLE

Today, we know of 118 elements.

Group 0 contains the noble gases. These are very stable elements that tend not to react with other elements.

The rows are called 'periods'.

Key

- Alkali metals
- Alkaline earth metals
- Transition metals
- Basic metals
- Semimetals
- Non-metals
- Halogens
- Noble gases
- Lanthanides
- Actinides

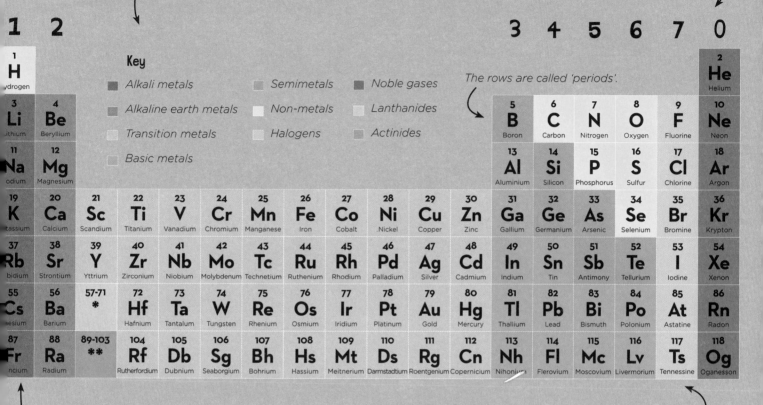

1	2												3	4	5	6	7	0
1 H Hydrogen																		2 He Helium
3 Li Lithium	4 Be Beryllium												5 B Boron	6 C Carbon	7 N Nitrogen	8 O Oxygen	9 F Fluorine	10 Ne Neon
11 Na Sodium	12 Mg Magnesium												13 Al Aluminium	14 Si Silicon	15 P Phosphorus	16 S Sulfur	17 Cl Chlorine	18 Ar Argon
19 K Potassium	20 Ca Calcium	21 Sc Scandium	22 Ti Titanium	23 V Vanadium	24 Cr Chromium	25 Mn Manganese	26 Fe Iron	27 Co Cobalt	28 Ni Nickel	29 Cu Copper	30 Zn Zinc		31 Ga Gallium	32 Ge Germanium	33 As Arsenic	34 Se Selenium	35 Br Bromine	36 Kr Krypton
37 Rb Rubidium	38 Sr Strontium	39 Y Yttrium	40 Zr Zirconium	41 Nb Niobium	42 Mo Molybdenum	43 Tc Technetium	44 Ru Ruthenium	45 Rh Rhodium	46 Pd Palladium	47 Ag Silver	48 Cd Cadmium		49 In Indium	50 Sn Tin	51 Sb Antimony	52 Te Tellurium	53 I Iodine	54 Xe Xenon
55 Cs Caesium	56 Ba Barium	57-71 *	72 Hf Hafnium	73 Ta Tantalum	74 W Tungsten	75 Re Rhenium	76 Os Osmium	77 Ir Iridium	78 Pt Platinum	79 Au Gold	80 Hg Mercury		81 Tl Thallium	82 Pb Lead	83 Bi Bismuth	84 Po Polonium	85 At Astatine	86 Rn Radon
87 Fr Francium	88 Ra Radium	89-103 **	104 Rf Rutherfordium	105 Db Dubnium	106 Sg Seaborgium	107 Bh Bohrium	108 Hs Hassium	109 Mt Meitnerium	110 Ds Darmstadtium	111 Rg Roentgenium	112 Cn Copernicium		113 Nh Nihonium	114 Fl Flerovium	115 Mc Moscovium	116 Lv Livermorium	117 Ts Tennessine	118 Og Oganesson

The columns are called 'groups'. Each group contains elements with similar properties. Group 1 contains very reactive metals.

These elements are shown below the main table because they are some of the most recent to be discovered and because they make the table too long for most books!

Group 7 contains the halogens, which are very reactive non-metals.

57 La Lanthanum	58 Ce Cerium	59 Pr Praseodymium	60 Nd Neodymium	61 Pm Promethium	62 Sm Samarium	63 Eu Europium	64 Gd Gadolinium	65 Tb Terbium	66 Dy Dysprosium	67 Ho Holmium	68 Er Erbium	69 Tm Thulium	70 Yb Ytterbium	71 Lu Lutetium
89 Ac Actinium	90 Th Thorium	91 Pa Protactinium	92 U Uranium	93 Np Neptunium	94 Pu Plutonium	95 Am Americium	96 Cm Curium	97 Bk Berkelium	98 Cf Californium	99 Es Einsteinium	100 Fm Fermium	101 Md Mendelevium	102 No Nobelium	103 Lr Lawrencium

These are the actinides. Nearly all of these elements have been created in labs.

The atomic number.

One- or two-letter abbreviation.

94
Pu
Plutonium

Official name, often chosen by the scientist that discovered it.

The Big Thinkers

The periodic table is used by scientists daily, but it didn't arrive in the world fully formed. It was developed over centuries and, in fact, it's still growing today. Let's look at some of the magnificent minds that contributed to this Big Idea.

PLATO
c. 428–348 BCE

Plato was a philosopher in Ancient Greece. He seems to have been the first person to use the word 'element' to mean 'one of the simplest or essential components of which anything consists'. But Plato thought that there were only four elements: earth, water, air and fire from which everything else was made. This view of elements was also held by philosophers such as Aristotle and continued to be believed until the Middle Ages.

The first to try to make sense of it!

The ones who got the ball rolling!

ANTOINE AND MARIE-ANNE LAVOISIER
1743–1794 / 1758–1836

Married French chemists Antoine and Marie-Anne Lavoisier came from noble families and were highly educated. In 1789 they wrote the first modern textbook on chemistry, *Elementary Treatise on Chemistry*. It contained a list of 33 'simple substances', including oxygen, nitrogen, hydrogen and many other elements.

There were a few mistakes — the Lavoisiers' list incorrectly included light and heat. But the talented duo did show that water wasn't an element, and 23 of the elements they listed are recognized today.

DMITRI MENDELEEV
1834–1907

Dmitri Mendeleev was a Russian chemist. He created the first version of the periodic table we use, in 1869. Using cards marked with the name and weight of each element, he grouped elements with similar properties together in a table. He concluded (correctly, it turned out) that any gaps were places for elements that hadn't yet been discovered. He realized the properties of these undiscovered elements could be predicted simply by looking at their place in the table. As a result, he predicted the existence of germanium and scandium, among others. Genius!

Mendeleev's table has been adjusted over time but its basic form is the same today. The element mendelevium is named after him.

The one who put the pieces together!

The one who made more discoveries!

MARIE CURIE
1867–1934

The work didn't end with Mendeleev. Lots of scientists have since discovered and added elements to the table, including Polish-born chemist Marie Curie. She and her husband Pierre investigated **radioactive** elements. This was dangerous research; Marie eventually died from **radiation** poisoning. But during her long career she discovered two elements (radium and polonium), became the first woman to receive a **Nobel Prize**, then the first person to be awarded a second Nobel Prize; she also developed travelling X-ray machines for use in the trenches during World War 1 and became the first female professor of physics at the Sorbonne University in Paris. So, we can agree she did alright.

Will the periodic table ever be complete? Today, scientists discover new elements in labs, not in nature. Elements 95–118 in the table are synthetic (made from chemical processes created by humans). These elements are very unstable and costly to produce, but the search for more continues.

Everything revolves around the Sun

WHAT IS OUR PLACE IN SPACE?

Today, we know that Earth orbits the Sun, but this wasn't always the case. In fact, for centuries, some of the brightest minds believed in a geocentric universe.

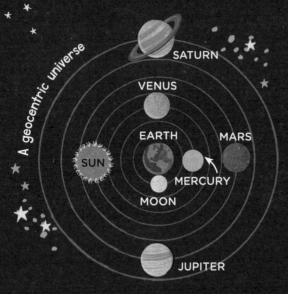

A geocentric universe

SATURN
VENUS
EARTH
MARS
SUN
MERCURY
MOON
JUPITER

WHAT IS **GEOCENTRIC UNIVERSE?**

The **geocentric** theory is that Earth is a fixed point in the centre of the universe that everything else moves around. This 'Earth-centred' idea came from the Ancient Greeks and was based on what they could see by gazing into space. Without telescopes, their guesses were often wrong. In this case, they were completely wrong... but that didn't stop people from believing it for more than a thousand years.

THE BIG DEBATE: GEOCENTRIC VERSUS HELIOCENTRIC

People wanted to believe Earth was at the centre of the universe because it made them feel that humans, and our planet, were more important than anything else. Eventually, a few brave astronomers challenged the geocentric theory by proposing that the Sun is at the centre of the universe, and that Earth and other planets **orbit** (travel around) it — this was called the **heliocentric** theory. Today, we know the truth: there is actually no central point of the universe! But Earth, the other seven planets and their moons DO orbit the Sun and we call our little patch of space the **solar system**.

STUFF AND NONSENSE

Ahem! It's the Sun, actually!

WHAT IS THE SOLAR SYSTEM?

Our solar system is made up of the Sun, eight planets (including Earth), moons, comets, asteroids, **dwarf planets** and lots of dust and gas. Everything in our solar system orbits the Sun because the Sun has the largest mass and has the most gravity (see **Big Idea 4**).

For a long time Pluto was considered the smallest planet in the solar system, but it is now classed as a dwarf planet.

This is the asteroid belt. Thousands, possibly millions, of smaller objects that are too small to be planets also exist here.

The four planets nearest the Sun are fairly small and rocky.

...he Sun ...ay seem ...lly big to ..., but in fact ...is just one of ...ndreds of billions ...f similar stars in our ...lky Way galaxy. ...e universe is filled ...th billions of ...laxies. So these ...ys, the idea that ...le old Earth ...uld be at the ...ntre of it all ...ems pretty ...likely.

MERCURY
VENUS
EARTH
MARS
JUPITER
SATURN
URANUS
NEPTUNE
PLUTO

Diagram not to scale

Jupiter and Saturn are gas giants, and mostly made of hydrogen and helium. Beyond them are the ice giants, Uranus and Neptune, which are mostly made from oxygen, carbon and nitrogen.

The Big Thinkers

The Big Idea of the solar system took centuries to get right. The notion that everything orbits the Sun, not Earth, was originally so unpopular that just by talking about it astronomers risked being arrested. Here are four fearless thinkers who stood by their theories — whether they had proof or not.

ARISTARCHUS OF SAMOS
c. 310–230 BCE

Aristarchus of Samos was an Ancient Greek astronomer and mathematician. He was the first to suggest that Earth orbits the Sun. He believed that fire was the best of the four elements (earth, water, air and fire), and that the centre was the very best position. So, he suggested that the Sun, which was made of fire, must belong in the centre of the universe. Although he was partly correct (the Sun *is* at the centre of our solar system — but *not* the entire universe), his reasoning was based on thoughts and feelings, not scientific proof — and his idea was ignored.

The one with the feelings!

The one who got it wrong!

PTOLEMY
c. 100–168 CE

Ptolemy was a Greek-Roman astronomer and mathematician. He proposed that Earth was a fixed point in space that the Sun and all the planets moved around. In his model of the universe (see page 16) the Sun was positioned between Venus and Mars. Unlike Aristarchus, Ptolemy really tried to prove his theories. He used maths to predict the movements of the planets and he described how a geocentric universe might actually work. It was all very complicated and seemed to be accurate... at least, without a telescope, which hadn't been invented back then. In the end, Ptolemy convinced his peers, and the geocentric theory was believed for over a thousand years. But we know today that he was totally and utterly WRONG.

NICOLAUS COPERNICUS

1473-1543

Nicolaus Copernicus was a Polish astronomer. He was obsessed with **astronomy** and he even built his own observatory! In his day, most people still believed Ptolemy's geocentric theory, but Copernicus wasn't convinced.

Like Aristarchus, Copernicus argued that Earth and the other planets revolved around the Sun. He spent more than 20 years researching, collecting evidence and writing his arguments for a heliocentric universe. Copernicus knew how controversial his theory would be and put off publishing his book until just before he died. He was right — his idea was hard to accept, especially for the Catholic Church, which saw it as **blasphemy**. Even a century later, when scientist Galileo Galilei (see page 22) supported Copernicus' theory, he ended up under house arrest for the rest of his life! Eventually though, Copernicus' idea was accepted. Go, Copernicus!

WANG ZHENYI

1768-1797

Wang Zhenyi was born in China at a time when girls didn't learn alongside boys. That didn't stop her! She educated herself and became a skilled astronomer. In her time, many people believed wild stories about things that happened in outer space. Some thought an **eclipse** meant a dragon had eaten the Sun! Wang Zhenyi wasn't one of them. She was into facts and science and she created a model to simulate and explain solar eclipses (where the Moon passes between Earth and the Sun) and lunar eclipses (where Earth passes between the Sun and the Moon).

Zhenyi died at the age of 29, but she achieved a lot! She mastered martial arts, horse-riding, archery and maths, as well as astronomy.

Facts about our solar system are still being revealed. In 2006 Pluto was reclassified as a dwarf planet, and Sedna, one of the most distant planet-like objects in the solar system, was only discovered in 2003. Temperatures there never go above -240°C. That's chilly!

What goes up... must come down!

WHEN YOU DROP A ROCK OFF A CLIFF, WHY DOES IT FALL TO THE GROUND? And when you throw your hat in the air, why does it come back down? These questions have been bothering humans for a very long time. So, what clever answers have we come up with?

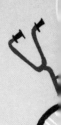

WHY DO THINGS FALL?

Aristotle, an Ancient Greek philosopher and scientist, believed that everything in the world had a natural 'place of rest' and this place was determined by what an object was made of. Aristotle thought that all objects would naturally seek out that place unless they were stopped by something hard, like a table, or a clifftop. He believed that rocks were mainly made of earth, so their place of rest was on Earth's surface and he thought this explained why falling rocks were attracted to the ground.

For centuries, people believed these ideas, but gradually scientists began to poke holes in this theory. After all, most things fall to the ground when dropped, not just rocks — pineapples, books, bicycles... and they're definitely not all made of earth.

Today, thanks to thinkers like Isaac Newton (more on him soon!) we know that things fall to the ground because of **gravity**.

WHAT IS GRAVITY?

Gravity can be described as a **universal force** that tries to pull objects towards each other. Every single object that has **mass** (anything made of matter, or 'stuff') exerts a gravitational pull. The more mass an object has, and the closer objects are to each other, the stronger the gravitational force is.

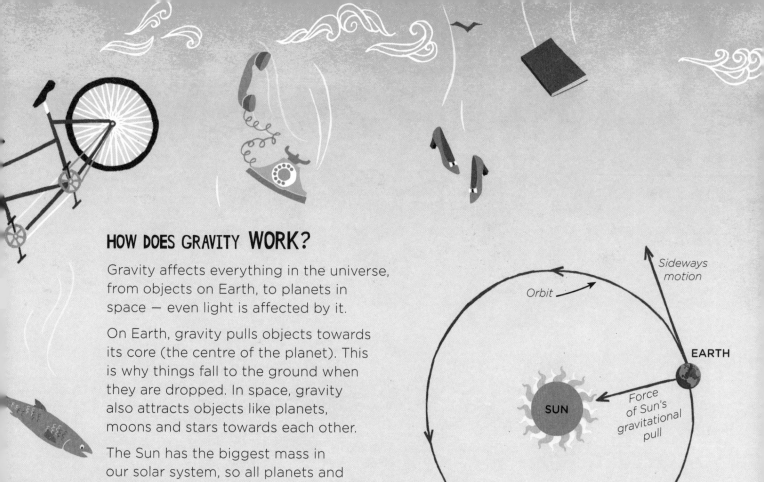

HOW DOES GRAVITY **WORK?**

Gravity affects everything in the universe, from objects on Earth, to planets in space — even light is affected by it.

On Earth, gravity pulls objects towards its core (the centre of the planet). This is why things fall to the ground when they are dropped. In space, gravity also attracts objects like planets, moons and stars towards each other.

The Sun has the biggest mass in our solar system, so all planets and moons are pulled towards it. But instead of hurtling right into the Sun and burning to a crisp, they orbit it. Why? Because the planets and moons are also moving sideways at great speed. The combination of attraction and forward motion causes orbits, and saves us from the massive fire ball in the sky. PHEW!

Orbit

Sideways motion

EARTH

SUN

Force of Sun's gravitational pull

All objects have a centre of gravity. This is the point at which gravity appears to act and is determined by an object's mass. For objects like Earth, which is a sphere, mass is evenly distributed all around, meaning the centre of gravity is right in the middle of it – at its core. This means that 'down' is always the centre of Earth, no matter where you are on the planet.

For objects that aren't spherical (like you!), the centre of gravity is not right in the middle of your body, it's usually slightly higher than your waist, as your top half has more mass.

The Big Thinkers

Gravity affects us every second of every day.
But for something that's so everyday, it's surprisingly
complicated. Let's look at a few of the scientists
who have tried to explain this tricky topic.

GALILEO GALILEI
1564-1642

Galileo Galilei was an Italian scientist whose studies included astronomy, physics and motion. He based his theories on evidence, not popular opinion. This got him into trouble while he was alive (see page 19), but today, he is celebrated as the father of the scientific method. Galileo was one of the first to carry out experiments to actually test his ideas. His experiments with falling objects (including dropping lead balls from the Leaning Tower of Pisa in Italy) led to important discoveries, including:

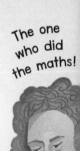

The one who dropped the ball!

• Objects with different masses fall with the same **acceleration**.

• **Friction** and **air resistance** are forces that slow things down.

But Galileo couldn't explain why things fall in the first place.

ISAAC NEWTON
1643-1727

The one who did the maths!

Isaac Newton was an English mathematician and physicist who was rather fond of cats. His contributions to physics, including his Laws of Motion, changed scientific understanding and are taught in science classes today.

Legend says that he saw an apple fall from a tree and realized that **a)** Earth was pulling it down, and **b)** the apple was also pulling on Earth, but its pull was weaker due to its smaller mass. Newton proposed that the two objects were mutually attracted, and he called this gravity. He went on to say that all objects with mass exert a gravitational pull and he used gravity to predict planetary movements such as orbits.

Newton's work was groundbreaking, but we know today that it wasn't entirely correct; his calculations didn't work for Mercury's orbit and didn't explain how things such as light — which has no mass — are also affected by gravity. It would take over 100 years for someone to get to the bottom of it all.

he one who changed the game!

ALBERT EINSTEIN
1879-1955

By the start of the 20th century, parts of Newton's theories on gravity weren't matching up with other discoveries in physics. German theoretical physicist Albert Einstein came up with a way to clarify things — in a very complicated way! In his theory of general **relativity**, he argued that gravity wasn't a force at all, but a change in the shape of **spacetime**.

Einstein proposed that space and time were connected, and he called this spacetime. Spacetime has form, like fabric or a sheet, and it changes depending on the objects within it.

This bending, curving and moving, Einstein argued, was gravity, and today scientists accept his theory. He also predicted the existence of **black holes** and **gravitational waves** (ripples in spacetime created whenever objects with mass move) — and he was right about that too.

However, most people still use Newton's laws for things on Earth, as they do work very well and are much simpler to understand.

Gravity can be understood by bends in spacetime. Imagine this grid is spacetime.

The mass of an object causes a curve beneath it and warps the shape of spacetime. The bend is always relative to the mass of the object. So, the bigger the mass, the bigger the bend in spacetime.

The most powerful benders of spacetime we know of are black holes. A black hole is formed after a star runs out of fuel and implodes. It collapses down to a tiny size but still has an enormous mass. This means its gravity becomes so strong it absorbs everything within its gravitational field, including other stars. Not even light can escape.

Objects like planets move through space in a straight line. When a planet enters the area of space warped by the Sun, the planet keeps following the same straight line, but because space is warped we see it swing towards — or be attracted to — the Sun. This also happens to light.

23

The universe is expanding

IF THERE ARE BILLIONS OF SHINING STARS IN THE UNIVERSE, WHY IS THE NIGHT SKY DARK? Good question! Our ancestors believed that stars were fixed, like painted scenery on a backdrop. Today, thanks to thousands of years of scientific enquiry, we know that:

1. There are 200 billion stars like our Sun in the **Milky Way** (our galaxy) and they're all moving.

2. There are billions of **galaxies** in the universe.

3. The universe is EXPANDING.

WHAT IS THE UNIVERSE?

The universe is HUGE. It's everything that exists, including you, milkshakes, the planets, even time! It contains billions of galaxies (groups of stars, gas clouds and dust particles).

Scientists have worked out that in the beginning the universe was teeny tiny. Then, the **Big Bang** happened and the universe has been rapidly expanding ever since.

HOW DO WE KNOW IT'S EXPANDING?

We know this because of **redshift** (this may sound like a nasty disease but it's actually all about light). Redshift is when light (which travels in waves) is shifted towards the red part of the spectrum (the range of visible colours humans can see) and this happens when a light-source is moving away. Scientists have observed redshift in light from galaxies, which means that these bodies are all moving away from Earth. But they're not zooming into empty space — it's the space between them that is stretching and getting steadily bigger. The whole universe is expanding from the inside out.

REDSHIFT

If a light-source is moving away from us, the light waves become stretched and shift to the red part of the spectrum. This is what happens to light from stars and galaxies.

WHY IS IT EXPANDING?

In 1998, astronomers came up with the idea of **dark energy** to explain the expanding universe. It's easiest to think of dark energy as the opposite of gravity, which pulls things together, whereas dark energy pushes things apart. Very little is known about dark energy but it is believed to make up 70% of the universe. It may be that this idea is spot on, but it could be totally wrong — we just don't know yet.

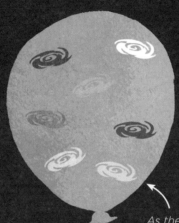

Imagine this balloon is the universe near the beginning of time. You can see that all the galaxies are close together.

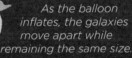

As the balloon inflates, the galaxies move apart while remaining the same size.

The more it inflates, the further apart the galaxies become. This is a lot like what happens as the universe expands.

SO, WHY IS THE NIGHT SKY DARK?

All this expanding helps explain why the night sky is not completely lit up by stars. You see, as the universe gets bigger, it causes the stars to spread out. As they get further away, their light has to travel much further to reach us and this means that they appear more dim.

The Big Thinkers

Scientists have been exploring ideas about the shape and size of our universe for thousands of years. Here are three of the brilliant brains that helped us figure out that the universe is expanding.

The one who computed the stars!

HENRIETTA SWAN LEAVITT
1868-1921

Henrietta Swan Leavitt was born in America and studied astronomy, at a time when men and women were not treated equally. Women were even forbidden to operate some telescopes. She knew she wouldn't be allowed to direct her own research, so after her studies, Leavitt did the next best thing... she got a job at Harvard University, US, as a 'human computer'.

Leavitt's task was to spend long hours analyzing pictures of the sky. She was researching Cepheid variables (stars that dim and brighten in cycles) and she discovered that the rate at which the stars faded and brightened was linked to their size and that allowed her to calculate their true **luminosity** (brightness). This enabled Leavitt to figure out how far away they were just by looking at them. Her work was groundbreaking — she had found an accurate way to calculate the distance of stars that were over 100 **light-years** away.

HUMAN COMPUTERS

For a long time, highly-skilled and mainly female scientists, mathematicians and cataloguers were employed as 'computers' by various academic and commercial organizations. Women took on this work because they were barred from leading their own research. Today, discriminating against women in this way is illegal in most countries.

26

GEORGES LEMAÎTRE
1894-1966

Georges Lemaître was a Belgian Catholic priest, a physicist and an astronomer. In his day, some scientists, including Albert Einstein, proposed that the universe was static, while planets and other objects within it moved around because of forces like gravity. But in 1927 Lemaître suggested that the universe was actually expanding and, he argued, if it was getting bigger, then perhaps it had once been very small indeed. He proposed that the universe originated from a tiny, ancient atom and has been expanding ever since a massive high-energy event. Later, in 1949, this process became known as the Big Bang, but in 1927, people weren't convinced. They thought Lemaître's theory was pretty 'out there' until a man named Hubble came along.

The father of the Big Bang!

The one who worked it out!

EDWIN HUBBLE
1889-1953

American astronomer Edwin Hubble is famous for discovering that the amount of redshift coming from a galaxy increases according to how far away it is from Earth. This is known as Hubble's Law. He used and studied the work of scientists like Vesto Slipher (an American scientist who first discovered redshift in bodies in space) and Henrietta Swan Leavitt to figure this out, eventually proving that the universe is expanding.

Hubble's discovery changed our view of the universe forever. In 1990, the Hubble telescope, named in his honour, was launched as an instrument for the entire scientific community It has since been used to study the accelerating expansion of the universe, which most scientists today attribute to dark energy.

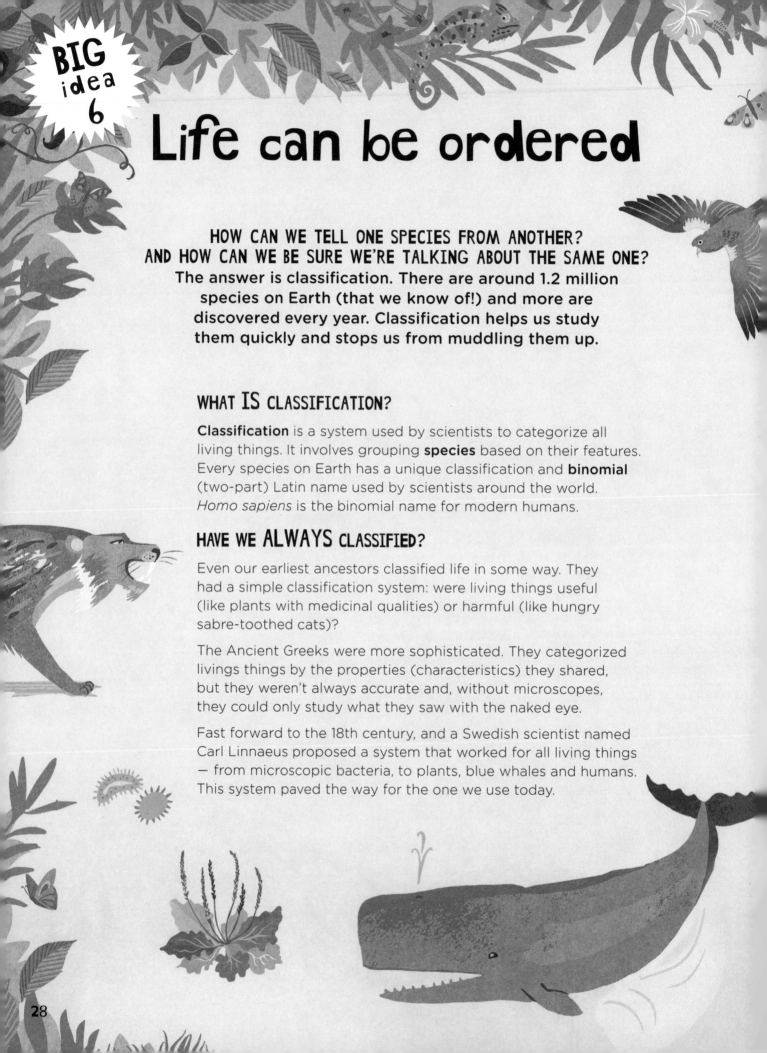

Life can be ordered

HOW CAN WE TELL ONE SPECIES FROM ANOTHER?
AND HOW CAN WE BE SURE WE'RE TALKING ABOUT THE SAME ONE?
The answer is classification. There are around 1.2 million
species on Earth (that we know of!) and more are
discovered every year. Classification helps us study
them quickly and stops us from muddling them up.

WHAT IS CLASSIFICATION?

Classification is a system used by scientists to categorize all
living things. It involves grouping **species** based on their features.
Every species on Earth has a unique classification and **binomial**
(two-part) Latin name used by scientists around the world.
Homo sapiens is the binomial name for modern humans.

HAVE WE ALWAYS CLASSIFIED?

Even our earliest ancestors classified life in some way. They
had a simple classification system: were living things useful
(like plants with medicinal qualities) or harmful (like hungry
sabre-toothed cats)?

The Ancient Greeks were more sophisticated. They categorized
livings things by the properties (characteristics) they shared,
but they weren't always accurate and, without microscopes,
they could only study what they saw with the naked eye.

Fast forward to the 18th century, and a Swedish scientist named
Carl Linnaeus proposed a system that worked for all living things
— from microscopic bacteria, to plants, blue whales and humans.
This system paved the way for the one we use today.

THE MODERN CLASSIFICATION SYSTEM

The modern system has seven categories into which all living things can be divided — humans too. Here's the classification of a giraffe:

There are five possible **kingdoms** in the modern classification system:

* animals (multicellular animals)
* plants (green plants)
* fungi (moulds, mushrooms, yeast)
* monera (unicelled organisms)
* protists (very simple organisms)

KINGDOM
Animalia (animal)

PHYLUM
Chordata (vertebrate)

CLASS
Mammalia (mammal)

ORDER
Artiodactyla (cloven-hoofed)

FAMILY
Giraffidae

GENUS
Giraffa (giraffe)

SPECIES
Giraffa camelopardalis

Humans can be classified too!

There is a fish known in English as the sarcastic fringehead. This name is funny but doesn't translate well. Classification gives it a name that everyone can use: *Neoclinus blanchardi.*

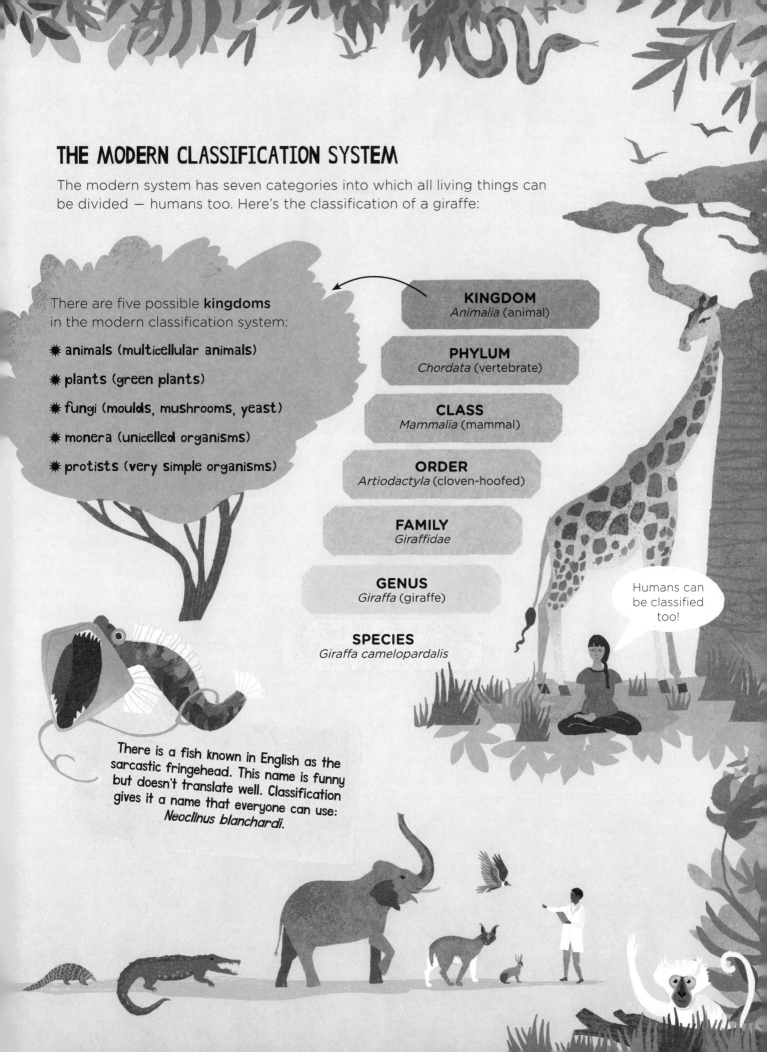

The Big Thinkers

Whether we're understanding extinct species or protecting existing ones for the future, classification plays a massive part in modern scientific study. So, who do we have to thank for this Big Idea?

CARL LINNAEUS
1707–1778

Carl Linnaeus was born in Uppsala, Sweden. He was into plants in a big way, and in 1732 he went to study the animal and plant life of Lapland in Finland. His findings formed the basis for his books, *Systema Naturae* and *Flora Lapponica*. In these books, Linnaeus used a system for classifying all living things, and introduced binomial naming.

Linnaeus' way of classifying **organisms** was based on similarities between them. For example, he looked at the teeth of mammals to see if species were related. His approach didn't falter when he got to classifying humans. Society at the time saw humanity as separate and superior to all other life on Earth, but Linnaeus categorized humans alongside apes.

Linnaeus' system was incredibly successful. A few changes and additions have been made over time, but after over 300 years it's still the basis for the system that scientists use today.

The one who grew the idea!

ARISTOTLE
384–322 BCE

Ancient Greek philosopher Aristotle was one of the first to classify living things. He sorted animals according to the colour of their blood, how they moved and how they were born. In Aristotle's system, butterflies ended up in the same group as birds and bats — which, as you've probably guessed, is not correct. But we can forgive Aristotle for getting this wrong because:

- Life is complicated. It often doesn't fit into one obvious category.

- Aristotle didn't have a microscope.

The one who planted the seeds!

ROBERT WHITTAKER
1920–1980

Both Linnaeus and Aristotle based their systems on what they could see, and they both divided life between two kingdoms: animals and plants. As science and technology developed, scientists were able to discover and study smaller and smaller organisms. In 1969, Robert Whittaker, an American ecologist, proposed that there are in fact FIVE kingdoms. He argued that fungi, bacteria and protists each needed their own category because they had unique cell structures and characteristics that did not exist in either plant or animal kingdoms. He was right, and the system was amended to the frankly awesome version we use today.

The one who branched out!

Classification isn't fixed. Some scientists argue for more kingdoms, and many classifications of species are disputed among experts. Advances in DNA testing are also leading to the reclassification of some species. But Linnaeus' basic idea remains in use.

Species change over time

WHERE DO HUMANS COME FROM? WHAT IS OUR CONNECTION WITH ALL OTHER LIVING THINGS? Some Ancient Greeks thought all living things just spontaneously appeared; others thought humans were hatched from prehistoric fish! Today, scientists believe the answers lie in evolution.

WHAT EXACTLY IS EVOLUTION?

Evolution explains how and why **species** change over time. Scientists believe that all the species in the world originally came from simple life forms (such as bacteria) and that over billions of years these life forms evolved to form all the **microorganisms**, fungi, plants, animals and humans on the planet today.

But why did they evolve? Charles Darwin (more on him very soon!) believed the answer was variation and competition. In his scientific theory of **natural selection**, Darwin highlighted how individuals within a species shared many similarities but also had many different characteristics — he called this 'variation'. He also noticed that every living thing was in competition for survival.

The winners of this competition were those with certain characteristics (sharp horns, long necks or big eyes, for example) that made them more suited to their environment and so better adapted to survive and pass on those characteristics to offspring. The losers died out.

With time, useful characteristics become more and more common and a species gradually changes. If enough time goes by, these changes can add up and an entirely new species can evolve.

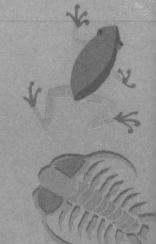

IS THERE **EVIDENCE** OF EVOLUTION?

Several clues make scientists confident that evolution is the answer, including:

The abbreviation for 'million years ago' is: MYA

FOSSILS: By studying fossils, scientists get a detailed picture of **extinct** species like dinosaurs. In certain cases, such as horses, they can trace the changes that have led to present-day species.

60 MYA   40 MYA   30 MYA   10 MYA   1 MYA

FORM AND FUNCTION: By studying human and animal **anatomy** we can see that many animals share certain useful bits. Humans, cats, whales and bats may look VERY different but their bone structure is similar enough that scientists say it indicates they all evolved from a **common ancestor**.

HUMAN   CAT   WHALE   BAT

DIRECT OBSERVATION: Evolution is usually a process that happens slowly (normally over thousands of years). But there are instances that we can observe. Microorganisms like bacteria can evolve quickly. Some are currently evolving a resistance to **antibiotic** drugs.

Dig Site

The Big Thinkers

The theory of evolution has forever changed how humans see themselves and the world around them. Understanding how evolution works can help us tackle parasites and combat disease-causing organisms. Here are some of the forward thinkers who helped us reach this point.

ANAXIMANDER
c. 610–546 BCE

Anaximander was a Greek philosopher who was interested in where living things came from. For him, the answer was a weird soup-like substance he called the *apeiron*. He thought it was the source of all life and that fish-like animals emerged from it. Inside these animals, the first humans took form and were held prisoners until puberty, at which point the fish burst open and died, and the humans came out!

It seems a bit fishy to us, too. But don't write him off entirely. With his idea, Anaximander had suggested an answer for how we might have become us, thousands of years before evolution was understood.

The one with the fishy idea!

The fossil hunter!

MARY ANNING
1799–1847

Mary Anning was an English fossil hunter. Captivated by the amazing clues about Earth's history, Anning began collecting fossils from age 12. Over the years, she discovered a number of fossilized ancient skeletons, including the first ichthyosaur skeleton. Her discoveries made the scientific community question how animals had changed over time, and led many to ask, 'Why?' In a few short years, answers would begin to emerge.

Anning often searched for fossils with her pet dog, Tray.

CHARLES DARWIN AND ALFRED RUSSEL WALLACE
1809–1882 / 1823–1913

Charles Darwin grew up in England with a passion for nature. In 1831, aged 22, he began a five-year expedition around the world aboard a ship called HMS *Beagle*. His mission was to observe and collect wildlife specimens and his studies led him to question how species change over time. After the voyage, Darwin worked to find the answers. In 1837, he wrote: 'One species does change into another'. Three years on, he had a theory for how this worked — but he spent nearly 20 more years gathering evidence.

Meanwhile, another British naturalist, Alfred Russel Wallace, also wished to study nature. In 1848 he boarded a ship, the *Mischief*, to collect specimens from the Amazon rainforest in Brazil. Like Darwin, he questioned how species change, and why, and by 1858 he had his own theory.

Knowing of Darwin's interest, Wallace explained his theory and sent it to Darwin. They had reached the same conclusion independently. Both had come up with the theory of natural selection — where helpful characteristics are carried forward from one generation to the next.

Darwin set up a reading of both of their papers in London, England, but there wasn't much of a reaction. A year later, in 1859, Darwin published his book *On the Origin of Species*. The book attracted huge interest, and controversy, because it contradicted religious teachings. Sadly, Wallace was rather forgotten.

Evolution is happening NOW: in petri dishes, in our bodies and in nature. In many cases, humans cause evolution. By taking more land and forcing animals out of their natural habitats, or attempting to kill them with chemicals, humans are inadvertently pushing them to evolve or die out. Bedbugs, for instance, have evolved in the last few decades to resist pesticides.

Bacteria cause infectious disease

WHAT CAUSES DISEASE? We know today that most diseases are caused by bacteria and viruses. But we didn't always have the answers! For a long time our ancestors thought the culprit was miasma.

FROM MIASMA TO BACTERIA

The 'miasma theory' was first proposed in ancient times. It suggested that illness was caused by clouds of bad air, called miasma. This bad air made people sneezy, spluttery and snotty. Sometimes it caused boils, bleeding, fever, and ultimately, death. This may sound a bit far-fetched to us now, but belief in miasma continued in Europe and China right up to the 19th century.

By that point, things were getting desperate. The **Industrial Revolution** meant people from the countryside flocked to the towns and cities where they lived in crowded and dirty conditions. Now, thousands of people were dying from diseases. Authorities tried to reduce miasma but the deaths continued. They began to wonder, if miasma wasn't the cause, then what was?

The answer lay in the past, in the late 1600s. The microscope had just been invented and when scientists used this new technology, they discovered **microorganisms** (tiny life forms). These life forms were often found in dead bodies and, at the time, many believed they were another result of miasma. But in the 19th century, scientists reconsidered. They realized that certain microorganisms, such as **bacteria**, were actually the cause of diseases and that miasma didn't really exist. By the end of the 19th century, scientists had realized that **viruses** cause diseases, too.

WHAT ARE BACTERIA AND VIRUSES?

Bacteria and viruses both cause disease. They're tiny,
and we can't see them without using a microscope,
but they're all around us, all the time.

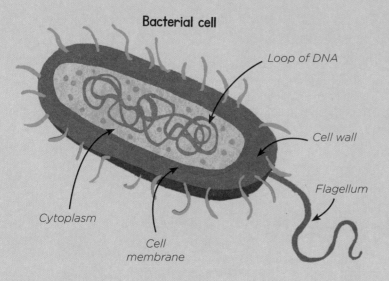

Bacterial cell

Loop of DNA

Cell wall

Flagellum

Cytoplasm

Cell
membrane

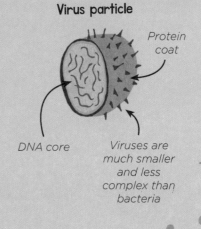

Virus particle

Protein
coat

DNA core

Viruses are
much smaller
and less
complex than
bacteria

Some bacteria are 'good' and help us stay
alive. But others are bad and carry diseases, like
tuberculosis. Viruses also cause diseases, such
as measles and flu. When we have a bacterial
infection, the bad bacteria multiply and attack
our healthy cells. When we have a viral infection,
the virus invades our cells in order to reproduce.
Basically, both are pretty nasty.

Today, we know that we can protect our bodies,
animals and food through:

AHCHOO!

* **Antibiotics:** Medicines that kill or slow
  the growth of bacteria.

* **Vaccination:** Injections that protect
  from viral and bacterial disease.

* **Sterilization:** Disinfecting or
  eliminating all microorganisms from
  a substance.

* **Pasteurization:** Heating foods
  (like milk) to eliminate bacteria.

* **Good hygiene:** Keeping hands clean
  and trying not to sneeze on each other.

The Big Thinkers

Now we know that bacteria are microscopic organisms that can cause infectious diseases, let's take a look at four big thinkers who helped this Big Idea burst into life.

The one with the principles!

HIPPOCRATES
c. 460–370 BCE

The Greek physician Hippocrates is considered to be the father of medicine in the Western world. He was the first to write about medical ethics and today's physicians follow many of the principles he introduced. Unlike his contemporaries (who believed diseases were created by angry gods and goddesses) Hippocrates was pretty sure diseases originated here on Earth. He wasn't entirely right though — he thought they were caused by wafting clouds of miasma.

The one with the data (and the lamp)!

FLORENCE NIGHTINGALE
1820–1910

Florence Nightingale was a British nurse. When war broke out in Crimea in 1853, she travelled to Turkey to care for British soldiers. Conditions were filthy: there were fleas and rats everywhere and more soldiers died from disease than from battle wounds. Florence collected data on deaths at the hospital. She then used her data to show that good hygiene reduced deaths. She pushed for reforms that saved lives. Her work, and the image of her alone with a lamp, nursing the wounded, is legendary.

LOUIS PASTEUR

1822–1895

Louis Pasteur was a French microbiologist whose work changed science and saved lives.

One of his famous experiments involved boiling and cooling some broth and then storing it in a swan-neck flask. The results were amazing — usually, after a few days, broth would go mouldy and bad, but this batch was still fresh. By boiling the broth, Pasteur had removed any initial bacteria (we call this process **pasteurization**) and by using a flask that limited air exposure, he prevented other bacteria from falling into it. He had worked out how to kill bacteria and make food and drink safer to consume.

Pasteur also studied **vaccination**. He worked out that exposing animals to weakened strains of a disease could be used to develop the animal's **immunity**, so they would not contract the full-blown version. This was BIG! Today, many children are vaccinated to protect them from diseases such as measles and tuberculosis.

The one who went hot and cold!

ROBERT KOCH

1843–1910

Robert Koch was a German microbiologist. He was researching bacteria at the same time as Pasteur (the two were said to be in competition). Koch found ways to stain, identify and photograph different microorganisms, and he was one of the first to argue that bacteria caused disease. He was awarded a **Nobel Prize** for identifying the specific bacterium that causes tuberculosis, a discovery that has saved countless lives. He also came up with 'Koch's postulates' (a set of four standards that can be used to prove whether a particular bacterium causes a particular illness) with his colleague Friedrich Loeffler. Today, we still rely on these standards to confirm causes of infectious disease.

The one who made the link!

The human body is full of bacteria. We need the majority of them to keep us healthy.

It's all in the genes

WHAT MAKES YOU, YOU? Our early ancestors realized that children often grew up to look and act like their parents (for better or worse!). But they had no idea why. Today we know that two things — environment and inheritance — influence how we turn out and the characteristics we have.

ENVIRONMENT AND INHERITANCE

Characteristics we get from our environment include things such as language, haircuts or scars. The characteristics we **inherit** include eye colour, nose shape and the shape of our earlobes (are yours attached?). But how do we inherit these things from our parents? Well, it's all down to our **genes**.

SO, WHAT ARE GENES EXACTLY?

Genes are pretty tricky to explain — first you need to know what **cells**, **chromosomes** and **DNA** are. Ready? Here we go...

1. All life forms are made up of cells (the building blocks of all living things). Humans are multicellular, meaning we are made of lots and lots of cells, not just one. There are 200 different types of cell in the human body and each type looks very different.

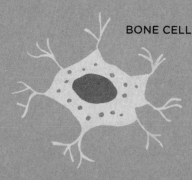
BONE CELL

LIVER CELL

FAT CELL

2. Most human cells contain a **nucleus** and this contains chromosomes. Most people have 46 chromosomes, 23 inherited from their mother and 23 from their father. Chromosomes are made up of long strands of tightly coiled deoxyribonucleic acid, or DNA for short.

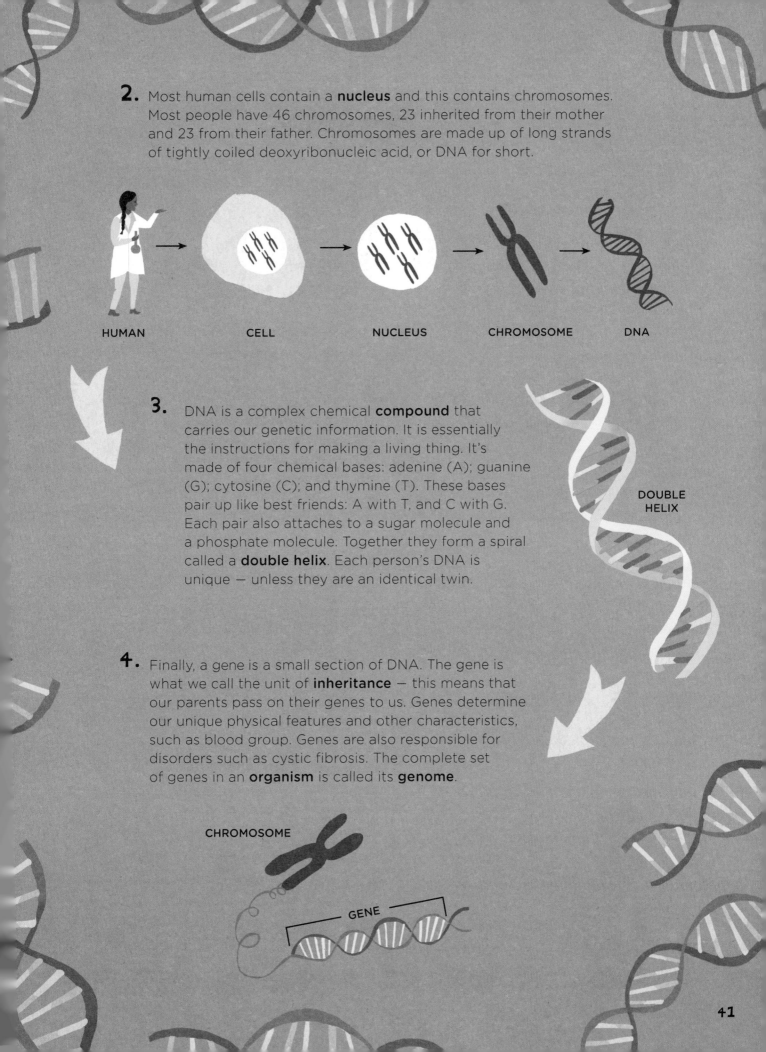

HUMAN   CELL   NUCLEUS   CHROMOSOME   DNA

3. DNA is a complex chemical **compound** that carries our genetic information. It is essentially the instructions for making a living thing. It's made of four chemical bases: adenine (A); guanine (G); cytosine (C); and thymine (T). These bases pair up like best friends: A with T, and C with G. Each pair also attaches to a sugar molecule and a phosphate molecule. Together they form a spiral called a **double helix**. Each person's DNA is unique — unless they are an identical twin.

DOUBLE HELIX

4. Finally, a gene is a small section of DNA. The gene is what we call the unit of **inheritance** — this means that our parents pass on their genes to us. Genes determine our unique physical features and other characteristics, such as blood group. Genes are also responsible for disorders such as cystic fibrosis. The complete set of genes in an **organism** is called its **genome**.

CHROMOSOME

GENE

The Big Thinkers

The discovery of genes, and DNA, has been called the most important of the 20th century. It has led to an entirely new science — genetics — and it has enabled us to understand and sometimes treat inherited disorders. Here are six superb scientists who played crucial roles in the development of this Big Idea.

ROBERT HOOKE
1635–1703

Robert Hooke was an English physicist, architect, astronomer, artist and biologist (an all-round genius!). He was also the first person to discover and describe cells. When Hooke looked at a piece of cork under a microscope he saw that it was made up of lots of tiny chambers — these were the cell walls in the cork tissue. They reminded him of the rooms where monks slept, so he called them 'cells'. His descriptions paved the way for cell biology and the discovery of what lay within cells — DNA.

The one who looked closer!

GREGOR MENDEL
1822–1884

Gregor Mendel was an Austrian monk who ran experiments on pea plants. He studied seven **traits** (or characteristics), including flower colour, and he noticed some fascinating patterns. In one experiment, he bred a red-flowering plant with a white-flowering one and found that all the offspring produced red flowers. He argued that this happened because the red flower trait was dominant, and so overrode the recessive white trait. After studying nearly 30,000 pea plants, Mendel concluded that all living things (including humans) pass down characteristics to their offspring. He called what was passed down the 'unit of inheritance' — today we call it a gene. Mendel's work was ignored in his lifetime, but today he is seen as the father of genetic science.

The one with the peas!

FRIEDRICH MIESCHER
1844–1895

In 1869, Swiss biologist Friedrich Miescher became the first person to discover DNA — though he called it 'nuclein'. He found it when he extracted the chemicals from the nuclei of white blood cells (which he collected from pus-filled bandages). It would be a full century before scientists realized what DNA actually did.

The one with the pus!

ROSALIND FRANKLIN
1920–1958

Rosalind Franklin wanted to be a scientist from the age of 15. She succeeded, and after going to university she worked in a lab producing **X-ray photographs** of DNA, in order to understand its structure. One of her team's photographs — 'Photo 51' — fell into the hands of fellow researchers James Watson and Francis Crick (see below). The photograph helped Watson and Crick work out the structure of DNA and produce the first model of it. Watson and Crick received a **Nobel Prize** for the discovery, but Franklin's contribution was forgotten. Now, scientists acknowledge that, without Franklin and her team, Watson and Crick may never have worked it out.

The one who got the shot!

JAMES WATSON AND FRANCIS CRICK
1928–present / 1916–2004

American biologist James Watson and British physicist Francis Crick wanted to understand and build the structure of DNA. In 1953, after months of gathering information, performing experiments, and with the help of Franklin's photo, they proposed that DNA's structure is in the form of a double helix. They built a model to demonstrate it and after seven years of defending their work they had enough evidence to prove it. Today, their discovery is world famous.

The ones who built it!

Energy cannot be created or destroyed

WHERE DO WE GET ENERGY FROM? Energy is everywhere. We've learned how to use it, but for centuries no one knew how it worked, or how much of it existed. Today, thanks to a few scientists, we have the answers.

SO, WHAT IS ENERGY?

Scientists define **energy** as the ability to do **work**. Energy is what makes things happen. It lights our homes, cooks our food — it takes energy to lift weights or hold this book. Many different forms of energy exist.

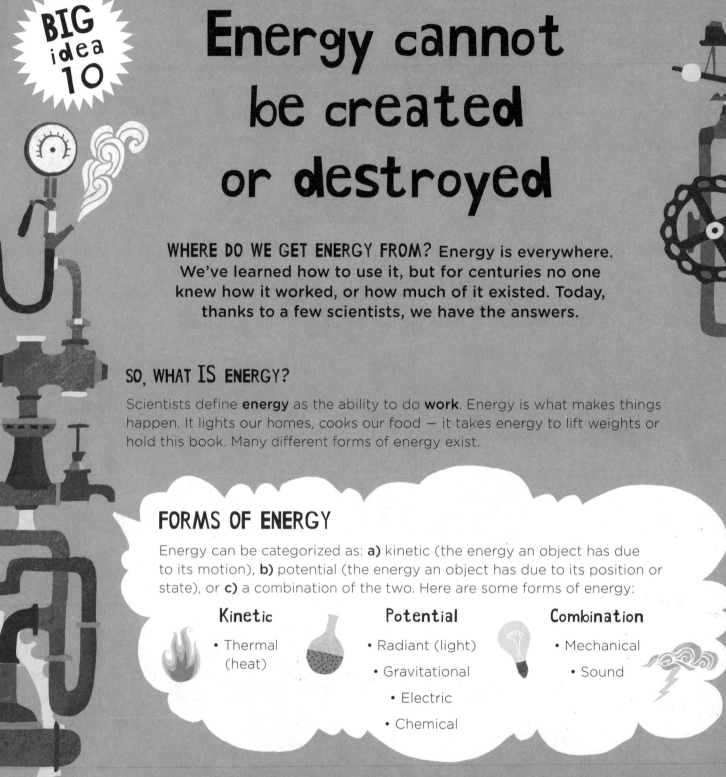

FORMS OF ENERGY

Energy can be categorized as: **a)** kinetic (the energy an object has due to its motion), **b)** potential (the energy an object has due to its position or state), or **c)** a combination of the two. Here are some forms of energy:

Kinetic
- Thermal (heat)

Potential
- Radiant (light)
- Gravitational
- Electric
- Chemical

Combination
- Mechanical
- Sound

THE LAW OF CONSERVATION OF ENERGY

In the 19th century, some clever scientists realized that energy can change from one form to another. They worked out what we now call the 'law of conservation of energy' (also called the 'first law of **thermodynamics**'). According to this law, energy can never be created or destroyed, it can only be transformed.

What's more, the total amount of energy in a closed system doesn't change. Our universe is a closed system, which means that the total amount of energy in the universe always stays the same, no matter how many times the energy transforms.

NEWTON'S CRADLE

This simple frame is used to demonstrate energy conservation. (It wasn't invented by Isaac Newton, but named for him.)

Nearly all usable energy comes from the Sun.

When ball 1 is lifted, it gains gravitational potential energy

Ball 5 swings up to almost the same height as ball 1 was originally lifted to

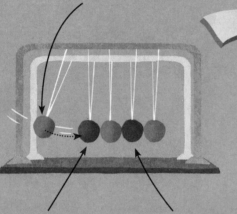

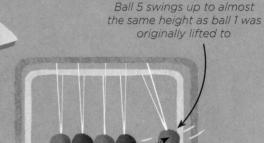

When released, ball 1 strikes ball 2, which remains still

The energy transforms and passes through balls 2, 3 and 4 as kinetic energy

The energy transforms back to gravitational potential energy

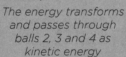

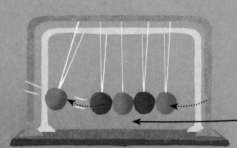

Ball 5 then swings back down, hitting balls 4, 3 and 2 with the same force as before, and ball 1 swings up again

According to the law of conservation of energy, this reaction should continue forever, but it doesn't because it's not a closed system. Energy escapes as sound and heat. Add to that the effect of friction as the balls strike each other. Eventually the balls will slow to a complete stop.

The Big Thinkers

The law of conservation of energy has led to many breakthroughs, from steam trains to refrigerators. Here are some of the pioneers who contributed to this Big Idea, from the ancient thinker who laid the foundations, to the heroes who cracked it.

EMPEDOCLES
c. 490–430 BCE

The one who paved the way!

Empedocles was an Ancient Greek philosopher who thought that everything was made of a combination of four elements: earth, water, air and fire, and that the world was in a permanent cycle where nothing new could come into being and nothing could be destroyed. Things could only transform from one to another through rearrangements of their elements. He was wrong (we know now that all matter is made of atoms), but the idea of a permanent cycle would, in time, be applied to energy and help form the law of conservation of energy.

ÉMILIE DU CHÂTELET
1706–1749

Émilie du Châtelet was a French noblewoman. Whilst translating some of Isaac Newton's work (see **Big Idea 4**) into French she saw a way to relate Newton's laws of motion to energy, and during an experiment Émilie proved that the energy of a moving object is always equal to its mass x velocity (speed) **squared**. This calculation would later prove crucial to the law of conservation of energy. Émilie died when she was 42 and her contributions to science were dismissed by jealous peers. She was forgotten for more than 200 years, but today her work is remembered.

The one who was forgotten!

'If I were king... I would have women participate in all human rights...'

JULIUS VON MAYER
1814–1878

The one who was ignored!

Julius von Mayer was a German ship's doctor. At sea one day he noticed that frenzied, storm-whipped waves were warmer than flat, calm waters. He realized that the motion of the waves produced heat, and that the more motion there was, the more heat was produced. Fascinated, Mayer learned all he could about how energy was transformed. His studies finally led him to submit a paper in 1842 in which he declared that energy is indestructible and will always continue to be transformed from one form to another.

'Energy is neither created nor destroyed.'

Unfortunately, other scientists dismissed Mayer's idea. He was never credited for his work in his lifetime — James Joule got the credit in the end — but Mayer continued to contribute to science and his work is recognized today.

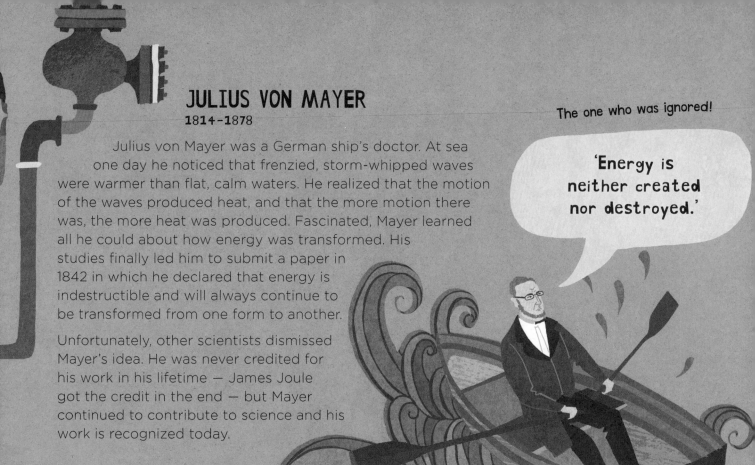

The one who got the credit!

JAMES JOULE
1818–1889

'Wherever mechanical force is expended, an exact equivalent of heat is always obtained.'

James Joule was born in England and grew up during the **Industrial Revolution** when new technology, such as steam trains, was emerging. He was interested in the science behind technology and he researched as much as he could. His experiments led him to find that the energy of mechanical work (like the force of lifting or dropping) and heat energy can be converted from one to the other. Joule also worked out that the amount of energy before and after conversion is always the same. Like Mayer, people dismissed Joule at first, but he soon convinced his peers and, today, it's recognized that his findings helped establish the law of conservation of energy. The international unit of energy is named the 'joule' in his honour.

Energy is transforming all the time: as we boil kettles, ride bikes or play the piano. Understanding the law of conservation of energy enables engineers to build more efficient machines, such as electric cars and trains.

Charged particles create electricity

WHAT DO EELS AND HAIRS THAT STAND ON END HAVE IN COMMON?

Electricity! Humans first encountered electricity thousands of years ago, but we only began to plug into what it is and how it works in the last few centuries. Now it powers our lives.

SO, WHAT IS ELECTRICITY AND HOW DOES IT WORK?

Electricity is a form of energy. It is created by the presence or flow of charged particles. All atoms contain charged particles: protons are positively charged and sit snug in the centre of atoms, and electrons are negatively charged and whizz around the outside of atoms.

Atoms of certain materials (such as copper and other metals) have looser-bound electrons, which can easily come free and move between atoms. We call these materials **conductors**. Electricity can pass through them easily.

Atoms in some other materials (such as glass, wool, plastic and rubber) contain electrons that tend to stay put. It's harder for electricity to pass through these. We call these materials **insulators** and we use them to protect us from being electrocuted (like the plastic covering of a plug).

FORMS OF ELECTRICITY

There are two forms of electricity:

1. Current electricity is the flow, or movement of **electric charge**.

2. Static electricity is the buildup of electrons on an insulator. It's called 'static' because the charges can't flow on, they stay in one area until they are discharged.

See Big Idea 1 for a refresher on atoms!

The bodies of electric eels contain electric organs that produce a charge that the eels can use to shock their prey.

Static electricity causes your hair to stand on end! This happens because the hairs are all the same charge so they repel each other.

OPPOSITES ATTRACT!

There are two different types of charge: positive and negative.

Objects with the same charge will repel each other.

Objects of different charge will attract.

WHAT'S SO **EXCELLENT** ABOUT **ELECTRICITY**?

Today, we control electric currents and harness electric energy to power things such as TVs, computers, trams... the list is endless. We do this by creating a circuit (a complete path) for the current to move around. A circuit always has to have a power source, such as a **battery**, a conductor (such as copper wires) for the current to flow through, and a device, like a lightbulb, that uses the electricity. These components all have to be connected for the current to flow.

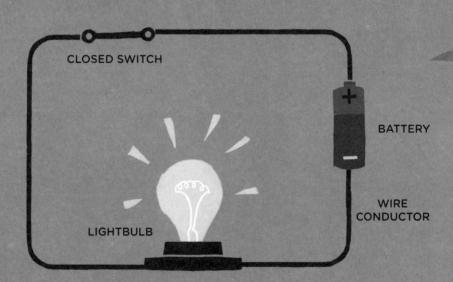

CLOSED SWITCH

BATTERY

WIRE CONDUCTOR

LIGHTBULB

ELECTRICITY + MAGNETISM = **ELECTROMAGNETISM**

In the 19th century, sparks were flying in the scientific community and lots of discoveries about electricity were being made. One of these discoveries was that electricity and **magnetism** (a force that is most powerful in metals such as iron and which causes objects to push or pull on each other) were linked. Scientists discovered that electricity could make magnetism and magnetism could also make electricity. So was born the science of **electromagnetism**. This science would lead to the first **electric motors**, **electric generators** and **transformers** — inventions that revolutionized the world.

The Big Thinkers

Throughout the centuries, a lot of people have contributed to the Big Idea of electricity. Here are four awesome electrical engineers who helped spark a revolution.

WILLIAM GILBERT
1544–1603

English scientist William Gilbert was personal physician to Queen Elizabeth I of England. He was interested in magnetism and wrote a book, *De Magnete* (meaning 'On the Magnet'), in which he showed that Earth behaves like a giant magnet. Gilbert also studied electrical forces and was the first to use the word 'electricus', which became 'electricity'. He did not, however, make the link between magnetism and electricity — in fact, like many of his day, he thought electricity was a kind of fluid. It took another 200 years before the idea of charged particles came along.

The one who named it!

The one who tamed it!

BENJAMIN FRANKLIN
1706–1790

Benjamin Franklin was one of the Founding Fathers of the United States (a group of men who helped North America become an independent country). He left school at age 10 when his parents could no longer afford it. He was curious about everything and read all he could. He found the science of electricity particularly fascinating and came up with the idea of positive and negative charge — a discovery that is used to explain electricity today. Franklin also realized that lightning was electric. He even proposed a dangerous experiment to test his theory: flying a kite with a metal key attached to it up into a thundercloud. He never tried it himself, but some scientists actually died attempting to carry it out.

⚠ DON'T TRY THIS AT HOME!

MICHAEL FARADAY
1791–1867

Michael Faraday was an English scientist who made many discoveries in electromagnetism. Despite leaving school at 14, he became captivated by science and taught himself by reading as much as he could. It worked and in 1821, a year after electromagnetism was discovered, Faraday created the world's first electric motor (a machine that converts electric energy into mechanical energy). Modern electric motors power all kinds of machines, from toothbrushes to trains.

Later, in the 1830s, Faraday worked out how to create electricity using magnets, a process called electromagnetic induction. His revolutionary discovery led to another two inventions: generators, which produce electric power through motion; and transformers — devices that transfer energy from one circuit to another and raise or lower the voltage in appliances, making them safer to use. That's a lot of discovering.

Faraday invented rubber balloons. He used them in experiments, not at parties!

The one who transformed it!

The one who simplified it!

EDITH CLARKE
1883–1959

Edith Clarke was a trailblazing American scientist. Orphaned at the age of 12, she went on to study maths, astronomy and electrical engineering. For a time she was employed as a human computer (see page 26); later, she struggled to get work as an engineer because she was a woman. Then, in 1921, she invented the Clarke Calculator, a device that could simplify the complex equations used by electrical engineers faster than any previous methods. A year later she became the first professional female electrical engineer in the United States. Way to go, Edith!

The author Mary Shelley was said to have been inspired by electricity when she wrote her famous novel *Frankenstein*, in which a scientist brings a corpse to life through a powerful force. Today, medics use electricity to save lives and restart people's hearts.

BIG idea 12

Fossil fuels WILL run out

WHAT WILL WE DO WITHOUT COAL, OIL AND GAS?
Since the Industrial Revolution of the 18th and 19th centuries, most societies have relied on these fossil fuels for heating, transport and power generation. But these resources impact badly on our planet, and what's more, they're running out.

WHAT ARE FOSSIL FUELS?

Fossil fuels are naturally occurring resources that formed over millions of years when the decaying remains of animals and plants were crushed by the rock and soil on top of them. It sounds pretty gross, but these fuels are incredibly valuable. When they are burned they release LOTS of usable energy.

Humans have been using fossil fuels for centuries. Ancient civilizations burned coal to stay warm, cook and light up the dark. Later, technology allowed us to mine for coal and drill for oil. Soon the world was consuming these resources in huge quantities.

There's a pretty important thing to remember about fossil fuels though: they're finite — once they are burned, that's it, they're gone for good. And these deposits take millions of years to form, so at the rate we are using them, eventually they'll run out.

AND ANOTHER THING

By using fossil fuels we are damaging the planet. Burning fossil fuels releases **carbon dioxide** and other gases known as **greenhouse gases**. As these build up, they trap heat from the Sun in our atmosphere and cause Earth to heat up. This is called **global warming**. As a result, polar icecaps are melting, sea levels are rising and extreme weather events are increasing — this is **climate change**.

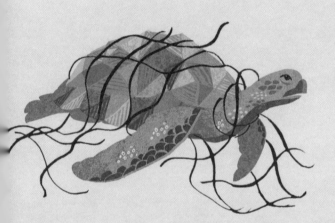

OH, AND ANOTHER THING

Most single-use plastics are made from fossil fuels. They are cheap to produce but doing so releases polluting chemicals. The disposal of plastic also poses a big problem. Much of it ends up in our oceans, where it harms precious marine life.

YIKES! WHAT SHOULD WE DO?

Don't panic and book your ticket to Mars just yet — there are other options. One is **renewable energy** (resources that will NEVER run out). These include **wind** and **solar power**. These sources can be more expensive and a little less reliable, but they don't cause as much pollution and they don't produce harmful greenhouse gases.

People have used renewable energy for centuries, but it's taken time to accept that burning fossil fuels adds to humanity's problems.

The Big Thinkers

Today, the world is getting much better at harnessing renewable energy. Let's meet some of the forward thinkers who have helped us understand the Big Idea that fossil fuels are finite, and renewables are the future.

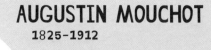

AUGUSTIN MOUCHOT
1825–1912

Augustin Mouchot was born in France and witnessed the **Industrial Revolution** in Europe. He believed that eventually fossil fuels would run out. He was struck by the idea that energy surrounds us whenever the Sun shines. If we could harness that, he thought, all our needs would be met! Mouchot spent six years developing a machine that used the Sun to heat water until it produced steam, which could then be used to drive turbines and generate electricity. Just as it seemed Mouchot's idea might be gaining support, the price of coal dropped, and people forgot about his machine. The world became hooked on fossil fuels, and Mouchot died in poverty.

The one who was ahead of his time!

The one who got the most wind!

POUL LA COUR
1846–1908

The Danish scientist Poul la Cour was not the first person to build a wind turbine for electricity generation, but his work helped make wind energy a realistic alternative to fossil fuels. He experimented with windmill design and found that, for maximum efficiency, windmills should have a small number of 'wings' that rotate at high speed. His findings were hugely useful, and these principles are still followed in the design of today's enormous wind farms.

SVANTE ARRHENIUS
1859-1927

The one who thought global warming was good!

In 1896, Swedish scientist Svante Arrhenius was the first person to describe how increased carbon dioxide emissions could cause global warming. Unlike today's scientists, he thought this was a good thing. He believed that warmer temperatures would prevent future deadly ice ages.

RACHEL CARSON
1907-1964

The mother of a global movement!

The desire to 'produce more than before, faster than ever' led to our dependency on fossil fuels. It also resulted in deforestation and the use of **pesticides**, which also have a negative effect on our planet. In her book *Silent Spring*, Rachel Carson, an American ecologist, described the devastating effects of synthetic pesticides on wildlife and the environment. She helped kickstart the environmental movement and bring these issues into mainstream thinking.

The one who interpreted the data!

CHARLES KEELING
1928-2005

Charles Keeling, an American scientist, spent 43 years studying and recording carbon dioxide emissions. His data demonstrated that increases in carbon emissions were related to increases in human activities, such as the burning of fossil fuels. He showed that humans were directly involved in the cause of global warming. Unlike Arrhenius, Keeling knew that this was NOT a good thing.

Today, people all over the world are working to tackle climate change, whether they're reducing their energy usage, investing in solar panels or recycling waste. Well done, humans. Keep it up!

Machines can solve problems

WHAT'S THE POINT OF MACHINES? To help humans! We've used machines to solve physical problems, such as moving heavy things (hello, crane) or popping corn (welcome, microwave) for some time. But analyzing information was always seen as the kind of problem only super-smart people could solve — until the computer came along and changed everything.

WHAT IS A COMPUTER?

You probably know what a computer looks like, how to use it and not to spill soup on it. You know it can help you do your homework, message friends or pass the time. But do you really know WHAT it is?

A modern-day computer is an electronic machine that stores and processes information.

WHAT KIND OF PROBLEMS DO COMPUTERS SOLVE?

Computers help us in countless ways, from reminding us of birthdays or connecting us with relatives, to helping us design skyscrapers or designer cars.

Computers can process vast amounts of data quickly. Before computers, when a government wanted to carry out a census (a survey of a country's population) it could take months, even YEARS, to sort the information by hand. In the 1950s, when the first computers were used, they could process THOUSANDS of entries in a MINUTE. Today's computers are billions of times faster.

SO **HOW** DO COMPUTERS DO THIS?

Computers don't solve our problems because they feel bad for us — no, they have to be programmed. A **computer program** is a collection of instructions that tells a computer to carry out a specific task — both what to do and how to do it, step by step. This flow-chart is an example of how to break down instructions like a computer programmer might:

A programmer wants the computer to recognize and decide when to close the boy's umbrella.

Computer checks if it's raining and makes decision: YES or NO

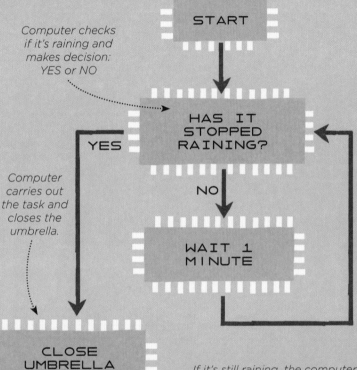

START

HAS IT STOPPED RAINING?

YES

NO

Computer carries out the task and closes the umbrella.

WAIT 1 MINUTE

CLOSE UMBRELLA

If it's still raining, the computer loops back and makes the decision again. This happens again and again, until the rain has stopped and the computer can carry out the task.

SPEAKING THE LANGUAGE

Computer programs are written in special programming languages and constructed using simple and specific commands. Computers don't understand human languages, including programming languages. They only understand a language called **binary**, which uses different combinations of the numbers 0 and 1. So even after a program has been planned out and written it still needs to be translated.

The Big Thinkers

We have lots of people to thank for the leaps taken by humankind in the field of computer programming. Here are just a few sensational software engineers we think you should know about.

ADA LOVELACE
1815-1852

Ada Lovelace was an English mathematician who was far ahead of her time. When she met computer pioneer Charles Babbage in 1833 she was keen to learn more about his Analytical Engine — a mechanical computer he was designing, capable of being programmed and storing data, much like today's electrical computers. Ten years on, and Babbage still had not built the machine (he never would) but Lovelace translated an article describing its workings. Her translation was far more detailed than the original and she added pages of notes, including a way to do complex calculations using the machine. This has gone down in history as the FIRST-EVER published computer program.

The first computer programmer!

As a child, Ada enjoyed designing flying machines. She wanted to build a horse with wings that could be steam-powered to fly.

The first to clarify computers!

GRACE HOPPER
1906-1992

American Grace Hopper was one of the first women in the world to gain a Ph.D. in maths. She believed that EVERYONE should be able to use computers — not just computer scientists. So, in 1944, she wrote the first-ever computer manual. In 1952, Hopper invented one of the first compilers (a program to convert computer language into binary). Her work led to the creation of a **programming language** that would become crucial to the world: COBOL (Common Business Oriented Language). Without it we wouldn't have traffic lights or air traffic control, and banking and healthcare systems would all fail. No wonder they called her 'Amazing Grace'.

ALAN TURING
1912–1954

Alan Turing was an English scientist and mathematician. In 1936, he came up with the idea for a Universal Machine, which could perform any set of instructions. His idea is recognized as the foundation of computer science. Turing went on to become a hero during World War 2, when he invented a machine capable of cracking the Enigma, a machine that created coded messages for the Germans. Turing was gay, which was illegal at the time. He was arrested and his genius was forgotten for many years. Today, he is recognized for services to his country and to science.

The father of computer science!

The first gamer!

STEVE RUSSELL
1937–present day

American computer scientist Steve Russell was part of a team that created one of the first video games. *SPACEWAR!* was created in 1962 and was a two-player game that centred on a dramatic fight between two spaceships. The joy and novelty of this game inspired future programmers and influenced the games we play today. The success of *SPACEWAR!* showed that FUN can inspire science and invention.

WEB OF GENIUSES
Every day, billions of us use the internet (a vast network of connected computers) to look at photos of cats and chat to friends. So who gave us this incredible gift?

VINT CERF (1943–present day) & BOB KAHN (1938–present day)
Pioneers of the internet, their work, the Internet Protocol (IP), paved the way for how the internet works today.

TIM BERNERS-LEE (1955–present day)
Inventor of the World Wide Web (a set of webpages on the internet). He made the internet something that EVERYONE could use for free.

Information is valuable

CAN WE USE INFORMATION TO BUILD A BETTER WORLD?
Humans have been generating and sharing information since they first appeared on Earth — about 66 million years ago! Today, humans generate so much complex information that we have a special name for it: BIG DATA.

WHAT IS BIG DATA?

'Data' is another word for 'information', and 'Big Data' relates to HUMUNGOUS amounts of data, of all different kinds.

?

HOW DOES IT WORK?

In the past, data was physical. It was books and papers, and humans would read and analyze it all themselves — armed with their brains and some pens and paper! Then, in the second half of the 20th century, people started using computers. New kinds of data appeared.

Today, every online news article, every social media post, every weather report or map we use contains data. And every time we like something, buy something or click on something online — we're also generating data. Then there's the 'Internet of Things' — a network of household objects, such as activity trackers or smart washing machines, that collect data about how many steps we take, or how many minutes to go until our socks are clean.

When you imagine Earth's 7.7 billion people all typing, clicking and searching, and all generating data, you can see why it's called BIG.

WHY IS BIG DATA VALUABLE?

All of this data isn't that useful on its own. But if it's gathered up and analyzed — then things become SUPER interesting. Because studying this data can help us understand and predict human behaviour. We call this science 'Big Data analytics', which is all about finding patterns and trends that scientists, businesses and services can use to make predictions, invent or improve products, and attract more customers. Essentially Big Data can be used to make things better.

THANKS TO BIG DATA:

- The security services can monitor all kinds of information to help keep us safe from fraud and other crimes.

  - Businesses can predict what customers may do or want next.

  - Customers can experience content that is tailored to them.

- Machines can be taught to learn without being programmed (see **Big Idea 15**).

PROCEED WITH CAUTION!

Though Big Data analytics can be great, it's always worth thinking critically — like a scientist. If adverts, articles or recommendations are always tailored, you only see or experience the same things over and over. This can stop you trying new things, hearing different viewpoints or varying your experiences. So, while Big Data helps us a LOT, it's important to remember its limitations.

71 872

84

5102

The Big Thinkers

From ancient libraries to smart watches, it's taken us thousands of years to accumulate all this knowledge. We're still working out what to do with it. Let's meet some of the daring data collectors who contributed to this Big Idea.

JOHN GRAUNT
1620–1674

Big Data as we know it only came about with the rise of computer technology. Before this, the job of analyzing huge amounts of information fell to regular humans. A British shop owner, John Graunt, was one of the first. Graunt lived in London at a time when the population of the city was rising incredibly fast. With rapid growth came challenges. Poverty and overcrowding caused disease and, for many, an early death.

The *London Bills of Mortality*, published weekly, listed all the deaths in London that week, as well as the cause of death. Graunt became fascinated by these figures. He decided to study and analyze them scientifically, to find patterns and draw conclusions about public health. In 1662, his findings were published in a book called *Natural and Political Observations made upon the Bills of Mortality* (not a very snappy title!). As well as highlighting the dangers of overcrowding and plague, it resulted in the first numbers-based analysis of the population of London. Graunt had founded the study of **statistics** as a scientific discipline.

The stats m

NIKOLA TESLA
1856-1943

Nikola Tesla was an American citizen, originally born in Serbia. He is remembered today as a world-changing electricity pioneer, inventor and scientist. But Tesla also made an exciting prediction about future technology. This is what he said:

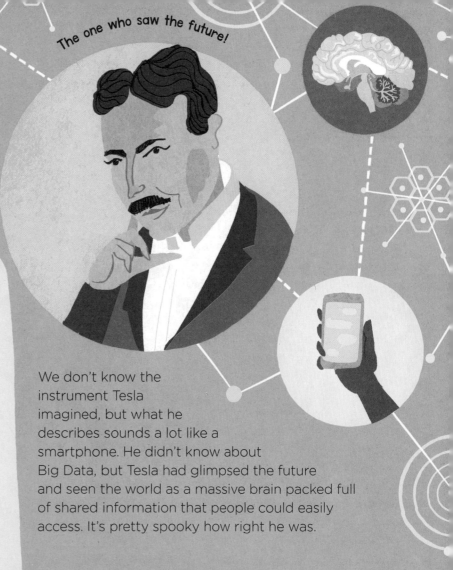

The one who saw the future!

'[...] Earth will be converted into a huge brain [...] We shall be able to communicate with each other instantly, irrespective of distance. Not only this [...] but we should be able to see and hear one another as perfectly as though we were face to face [...] and the instruments through which we shall be able to do this will be amazingly simple. [...] man will be able to carry one in his vest pocket.'

We don't know the instrument Tesla imagined, but what he describes sounds a lot like a smartphone. He didn't know about Big Data, but Tesla had glimpsed the future and seen the world as a massive brain packed full of shared information that people could easily access. It's pretty spooky how right he was.

Big Data is a thing of the present (and future) and, as we've learned, it's reliant on increasingly advanced computer technology to store and process it all. But humans were obsessed with collecting, sharing and learning from data LONG before it could be downloaded — they just did it physically, poring over manuscripts and books in libraries. These institutions have existed since ancient times. Their goal is to gather as much information as possible and share it freely in order to teach and inspire us. Today, data generation and analysis may have changed, but libraries are still important in society — check one out.

SHHH! OLD-FASHIONED DATA ANALYSIS IN PROGRESS.

Machines can learn

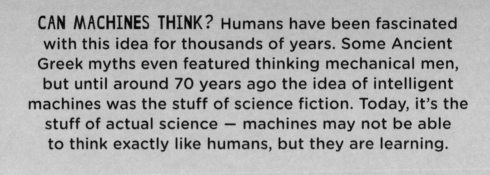

CAN MACHINES THINK? Humans have been fascinated with this idea for thousands of years. Some Ancient Greek myths even featured thinking mechanical men, but until around 70 years ago the idea of intelligent machines was the stuff of science fiction. Today, it's the stuff of actual science — machines may not be able to think exactly like humans, but they are learning.

WHAT IS **MACHINE LEARNING?**

First, we need to understand **artificial intelligence (AI)**. AI is the idea that machines could one day think for themselves and make decisions. It kicked off in the 1950s and hasn't stopped since. Advances have ranged from computers beating champion chess players, to gadgets such as smart speakers that remember your favourite song, right up to self-driving vehicles and machines that can differentiate between healthy and unhealthy hearts.

Machine learning is a branch of AI. It's a trial-and-error process, where a device runs a task billions of times, over and over again, storing and analyzing every piece of data it generates, in order to learn how to do it better the next time.

WHO'S MAKING THE DECISIONS?

Has your computer ever suggested the next book you might like to buy from a website? That's machine learning. The computer has analyzed data from the website and:

- Remembered what you bought before.

- Found patterns to establish what you like and don't like.

- Considered what other people who bought the same books as you have gone on to buy.

- Made a decision and recommended a new book.

That's pretty powerful. Imagine if computers used the same methods to suggest who you should vote for, or what to believe: would you listen to a machine?

HOW TO TEACH TECHNOLOGY

Say you want to teach a computer to tell the difference between a picture of a teapot and one of an elephant...

1. You could begin by feeding it lots of pictures of teapots and lots of pictures of elephants and simply telling it the answers.

2. You could write a series of yes/no questions about the features of each picture for the computer to answer and apply before giving its judgement.

3. You could use the internet to show the computer millions of pictures of teapots and millions of pictures of elephants and let it make its own conclusions based on previous correct answers.

4. You could work a feedback loop into the program so the computer logs when it gets the answer right and when it gets it wrong.

Over time, the computer would get better at telling the difference between a teapot and an elephant. In other words, IT WOULD LEARN.

The Big Thinkers

Lots of people have contributed to the Big Idea that machines can simulate humans and go on to learn and think for themselves. We think these individuals deserve special attention.

The one with the party tricks!

The one with the test!

ISMAIL AL-JAZARI
1136–1206

Ismail al-Jazari was an engineer born in modern-day Turkey. The little we know of him is from his *Book of Ingenious Mechanical Devices*, published in 1206. In it, he describes more than 100 of his inventions, including a robotic musical band and a mechanical waiter that served drinks (nifty!). It would take over 800 years until machines were capable of learning or imitating human thought, but al-Jazari's machines show that we have long been interested in creating mechanical versions of ourselves.

ALAN TURING
1912–1954

You read about Alan Turing in **Big Idea 13**, but he deserves a mention here, too. Turing never lived to see any examples of AI, but he did devise a test to measure machine intelligence based on whether a machine could fool a human into mistaking it for a person. He called the test 'The Imitation Game', though it's now known as the **Turing Test**. It's still used to measure AI today.

66

JOHN MCCARTHY
1927–2011

John McCarthy was the American computer scientist who came up with the term 'artificial intelligence'. In 1956, he organized a summer research project with the aim of studying AI. It was attended by various computer scientists, including Arthur Samuels (who coined the term 'machine learning'). After six weeks of research, discussion and planning, the scientists went on to contribute hugely to the field of AI, all thanks to McCarthy's summer camp.

The one with the summer camp!

The one who wrote the laws!

ISAAC ASIMOV
1920–1992

Isaac Asimov was born in Russia and later became a US citizen. He loved writing and was a successful science-fiction author. In one short story, he set out some laws for all AI machines to follow:

- **Law 1:** A robot may not injure a human being, or by inaction, allow a human being to come to harm.

- **Law 2:** A robot must obey the instructions given to it by human beings, except where such orders would conflict with the first law.

- **Law 3:** A robot must protect its own existence as long as such protection does not conflict with the first or second laws.

Asimov's laws made people think about the ethics (moral principles) of AI.

⚠ HOLD ONTO YOUR BRAINS!

IT'S GETTING COMPLICATED!

DEEP LEARNING

In 2011, computer scientists Jeff Dean, Greg Corrado and Andrew Ng founded a research team called Google Brain. Its mission is to make machines intelligent and improve people's lives. It does this using deep learning. Deep learning involves building ANNs (artificial neural networks) — systems designed to act like the human brain. ANNs are made of up thousands of interconnected computers, each programmed to act like a single brain cell. When given a task these cells work together. Processing data like this enables machines to learn more than ever and is changing our world.

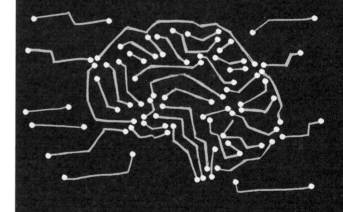

Future Big Ideas

This book has explored 15 brilliantly big science ideas, but that's just the beginning. Even as you read this, engineers, inventors, computer scientists and ecologists are busy working on ideas that might one day change our world. Let's take a look at some of the ideas that are being developed right now.

LIFE ON MARS

Earth is facing some big problems, such as climate change and overpopulation, so why don't we colonize other planets, like Mars? Sure, it's lonely, cold, there's no liquid water and the air is unbreathable, but apart from that, what's not to love about the Red Planet? In fact, scientists are working hard to put humans on Mars sometime in the next 30 years. For example, NASA's robotic lander InSight touched down on Mars in November 2018 as part of a mission to unlock the planet's secrets and figure out whether one day we might make a home there.

HOME

3D PRINTING MEDICINE AND FOOD

You've probably heard of 3D printing, but can you imagine eating a meal that had come from a printer, or printing your own medication, or how about bioprinting to make replacement body parts? All these amazing ideas are in development in labs around the world. This big idea has the potential to revolutionize the way we make, buy and sell things. If engineers are successful, we could decrease waste, reduce fuel use and save millions of lives in the process.

ROBOT TEACHERS AND PHYSICIANS

In the future, many tasks will be done by robots, but how about jobs such as teaching, or healing the sick? Robots may never fully replace humans in these jobs, but they can support human teachers and surgeons very well. In Japan, for example, robots are being tested in classrooms as teaching assistants. Robot teachers never get tired or lose patience, unlike busy, stressed-out humans. Likewise, surgical robots are not as likely to make mistakes, or get nervous.

INVISIBLE COMPUTING

Computers are disappearing. They're not actually going anywhere, far from it. Instead, engineers are working to make the next generation of devices invisible. In the future, instead of typing on a keyboard, you will talk to your devices or move through them.

Smart speakers, watches and phones are already here, but in time, your whole home could know how you like it heated, or lit or just how fluffy you like your pillows.

GIANT VIRUSES

We humans still don't know everything there is to know about the natural world. We used to think that all viruses were tiny and had very few genes — some are known to have as few as four — then we discovered giant viruses, which can be bigger than some bacteria, with about 500 genes. The sophistication of these viruses is making some scientists question previously believed ideas and could even lead to revisions in our understanding of the history of living things.

UPLOADING THE HUMAN BRAIN

Within the next 30 years, scientists think they will be able to upload the entire contents of a human brain onto a computer. What would this mean for the human race? Well, instead of dying when our bodies become too old, it would mean that our consciousness (all the information that makes us, us) could be uploaded to a machine and maybe transferred into a 'brand new' body at a later time, effectively making humans immortal. Is it possible? No one knows.

More big thinkers you should know about

This book has got some pretty awesome people in it, but there are thousands more who deserve your attention. With that in mind, here are some extra thinkers we know you'd love to meet.

Zhang Heng
78-139 CE
Chinese astronomer and inventor. He realized that the Moon reflects the Sun's light and is not a source of light itself.

Ibn al-Haytham
c. 965-1040
Arabic mathematician and physicist. One of the first to recognize that humans see when light enters their eyes.

Maria Sibylla Merian
1647-1717
German naturalist and artist. She studied insects and caterpillars and may have been the first person to draw the metamorphosis of a butterfly from observation.

Elizabeth Blackwell
1821-1910
British physician. The first woman to be granted a medical degree in the United States and a pioneering advocate for women's education.

Metrodora
c. 200-400 CE
Greek physician and author of the first medical handbook known to have been written by a woman.

Leonardo da Vinci
1452-1519
Italian inventor and artist. One of the first users of the scientific method. He studied anatomy, designed machines that would not be invented for centuries (such as helicopters) and painted masterpieces.

George Washington Carver
c. 1864-1943
American botanist. Discovered that growing nitrogen-rich crops, such as peanuts helps restore soil that has been heavily farmed.

Marie Maynard Daly
1921–2003
American biochemist. Helped to discover the relationship between high cholesterol and clogged arteries — a cause of heart attacks — saving countless lives as a result.

Stephen Hawking
1942–2018
British theoretical physicist. He predicted that black holes emit radiation, called Hawking radiation. His book *A Brief History of Time* helped introduce cosmology (the study of the universe) to mainstream readers.

Subrahmanyan Chandrasekhar
1910–1995
Indian-born American astrophysicist. His calculations led to today's understanding of supernovas, neutron stars and black holes.

Annie Easley
1933–2011
American mathematician and rocket scientist. Worked at NASA for nearly 35 years, first as a human computer, later as a programmer, helping to design the Centaur rocket.

Hedy Lamarr
1914–2000
Austrian-born American movie star and inventor. Invented a way for radio signals to hop frequencies, paving the way for Wifi.

Jane Goodall
1934–present
British scientist and conservationist. Discovered that chimpanzees make tools and behave more like humans than previously thought. Her work has revolutionized the study of primates.

Konstantin Batygin
1986–present
Russian-American astrophysicist and assistant professor. Researches the formulation and evolution of the solar system. Suggests that there could be a ninth planet very far out in our solar system.

David Attenborough
1926–present
British naturalist and documentary maker. His work has helped to highlight threats to the natural world, including global warming, loss of habitat and plastic pollution.

Mae Jemison
1956–present
American engineer and astronaut. She led many of NASA's science missions and was the first African-American woman to travel in space.

Timeline of BIG Science Ideas

This timeline doesn't capture every development in the history of science — that would be enough to fill this book! But it does show some interesting details, like which ideas developed at the same time...

6TH CENTURY BCE	5TH CENTURY BCE	4TH CENTURY BCE	3RD CENTURY BCE	2ND CENTURY BCE	DARK AGES	13TH CENTURY

c. **335 BCE Aristotle** says everything is made of air, water, earth and fire.

BIG IDEA 1: EVERYTHING IS MADE OF ATOMS

c. **400 BCE Democritus** argues that all matter is made of indivisible *atomos*.

Sometimes lots of big ideas happened at once, but sometimes not very much happened for quite a long time...

BIG IDEA 2: ELEMENTS CAN BE ORDERED

c. **360 BCE Plato** coins the term 'elements' to describe earth, water, air and fire.

c. **200 BCE Aristarchus** states that the Sun is the centre of the universe.

c. **130 BCE Ptolemy** argues that the Sun and planets orbit Earth.

BIG IDEA 3: EVERYTHING REVOLVES AROUND THE SUN

BIG IDEA 4: WHAT GOES UP... MUST COME DOWN!

c. **335 BCE Aristotle** states that objects move because of their properties, e.g. rocks fall to Earth because they are made of earth.

BIG IDEA 5: THE UNIVERSE IS EXPANDING

c. **347 BCE Aristotle** classifies animals according to their properties.

BIG IDEA 6: LIFE CAN BE ORDERED

c. **600–500 BCE Anaximander** suggests that humans hatched from fish.

BIG IDEA 7: SPECIES CHANGE OVER TIME

Turn the page to see the remaining Big Idea timelines.

KEY

BCE stands for 'Before the Common Era' and relates to all dates before the birth of Jesus Christ.

c. stands for *circa*, which means 'around'. It's used when a precise date is unknown.

15TH CENTURY	16TH CENTURY	17TH CENTURY	18TH CENTURY	19TH CENTURY	20TH CENTURY	21ST CENTURY

1803 John Dalton shows that atoms of one type share the same properties.

1897 J.J. Thomson discovers the electron.

c. **1789 William Higgins** develops an early version of atomic theory.

1911 Ernest Rutherford discovers the nucleus.

1898 Marie and **Pierre Curie** discover radium and polonium.

1789 Antoine and **Marie-Anne Lavoisier** compile a list of 33 elements.

1869 Dmitri Mendeleev creates the first version of the periodic table.

1543 Nicolaus Copernicus publishes his heliocentric theory.

1780 Wang Zhenyi explains eclipses.

1687 Isaac Newton uses gravity to explain orbits. But his calculations don't work for Mercury.

1589-92 Galileo Galilei shows that falling objects accelerate equally.

1915 Albert Einstein states that gravity occurs because mass bends spacetime.

1927 Georges Lemaître argues the universe began as a tiny atom and has been expanding ever since.

1912 Henrietta Swan Leavitt works out how to calculate the distances of certain stars from Earth.
1912 Vesto Slipher discovers redshift in bodies in space.

1929 Edwin Hubble uses redshift to prove that the universe is expanding.

1735 Carl Linnaeus describes a system for the classification of all living things.

1969 Robert Whittaker proposes the five kingdoms of life.

1811 Mary Anning finds the first ichthyosaur fossil.

c. **1850s Alfred Russel Wallace** and **Charles Darwin** both come up with the theory of natural selection.

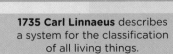

73

BIG IDEA 8: BACTERIA CAUSE INFECTIOUS DISEASE

c. **400 BCE Hippocrates** says that diseases are transmitted through bad air.

BIG IDEA 9: IT'S ALL IN THE GENES

c. **450 BCE Empedocles** says the universe is in a permanent cycle of growth and decay.

BIG IDEA 10: ENERGY CANNOT BE CREATED OR DESTROYED

c. **600 BCE Thales of Miletus** creates static electricity by rubbing amber with fur, causing it to attract light objects, like feathers.

BIG IDEA 11: CHARGED PARTICLES CREATE ELECTRICITY

BIG IDEA 12: FOSSIL FUELS WILL RUN OUT

BIG IDEA 13: MACHINES CAN SOLVE PROBLEMS

BIG IDEA 14: INFORMATION IS VALUABLE

1206 Ismail al-Jazari writes about his inventions, including a mechanical waiter.

BIG IDEA 15: MACHINES CAN LEARN

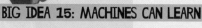

1660s Antonie van Leeuwenhoek is the first person to see microorganisms.

1864 Louis Pasteur develops pasteurization.

1854 Florence Nightingale champions good hygiene.

1877 Robert Koch says microorganisms cause disease.

c. 1850–60 Gregor Mendel discovers the basic principles of genetics.

1952 Rosalind Franklin photographs crystalized DNA fibres.

1665 Robert Hooke discovers and names cells.

1869 Friedrich Miescher discovers DNA.

1953 James Watson and **Francis Crick** describe the double helix structure of DNA.

c. 1840s James Joule experiments to find the mechanical equivalent of heat.

1740 Émilie du Châtelet shows that the energy of a moving object can be measured according to its velocity squared.

1842 Julius von Mayer writes the phrase 'Energy is neither created nor destroyed'.

1600 William Gilbert coins the term 'electricus'.

1921 Edith Clarke invents the Clarke Calculator.

1752 Benjamin Franklin says that lightning is electrical.

1821 Michael Faraday invents the first electric motor.

1866 Augustin Mouchot runs the first solar-powered steam engine.

1962 Rachel Carson publishes *Silent Spring*.

1896 Svante Arrhenius argues that increases in carbon dioxide contribute to global warming.
1899 Poul la Cour describes his ideal windmill for maximum efficiency.

1958 Charles Keeling finds that humans are connected to rising greenhouse gases.

1936–37 Alan Turing describes his 'Universal Machine'.

1962 Steve Russell and his colleagues create *SPACEWAR!*

1842 Ada Lovelace becomes the first computer programmer.

1952 Grace Hopper creates a compiler, to translate computer language into binary.

1662 John Graunt compiles a 'life table' and becomes one of the first people to study statistics.

1926 Nikola Tesla predicts that humans will be able to access data using a pocket-sized device.

1942 Isaac Asimov publishes the Three Laws of Robotics.

1950 Alan Turing devises the 'Turing Test'.

1955 John McCarthy coins the term 'artificial intelligence'.

Glossary

A

ACCELERATION a measure of how fast a speed is increasing, second by second.

AIR RESISTANCE a force that slows objects as they move through the air.

ANATOMY the structure of a living thing.

ANTIBIOTICS medicines that target microorganisms but do not harm healthy body cells.

ARTIFICIAL INTELLIGENCE (AI) a computer program that is able to think and learn.

ASTRONOMY the science of things beyond Earth, including the Sun, Moon and stars.

ATOM a tiny particle made of a number of even tinier particles. Atoms bond together to make all the things we see around us.

ATOMIC NUMBER the total number of protons in an atom.

ATOMIC THEORY the theory that all matter is made of atoms.

B

BACTERIUM (plural: bacteria) a tiny living thing with just one cell. Some bacteria cause illnesses; others help with body processes such as digestion.

BATTERY a device that creates an electric current from chemical reactions.

BCE stands for 'Before the Common Era'. The Western world divides time into two eras based around the birth of Jesus Christ. BCE relates to dates before this event.

BIG BANG the theory that the entire universe and everything in it began as a single point in space that exploded in all directions.

BINARY a numeric system that uses only two digits: 0 and 1. Computers work in binary.

BINOMIAL a naming system that gives everything two names. Living things are named in this way by scientists.

BIOLOGY the science of living things.

BLACK HOLE a very small but very heavy object in space that is formed when a star comes to the end of its life and collapses in on itself. Its gravity is so strong that nothing can escape its pull, not even light.

BLASPHEMY the act of speaking badly of or in contradiction to a religion.

C

CARBON DIOXIDE a gas made from carbon and oxygen. Carbon dioxide is produced when things burn.

CE stands for 'Common Era'. The Western world's calendar divides time into two eras based around the birth of Jesus Christ. CE relates to dates after this event.

CELL the building block from which all living things are made. Tiny living things have only one cell, but large organisms, such as humans, have trillions.

CHEMISTRY the science of materials and their reactions.

CHROMOSOME found in the cell nucleus, it carries genetic information and is made of tightly coiled strands of DNA.

C. (CIRCA) 'c.' stands for *circa*, which means 'around'. It's used when a precise date is unknown.

CLASSIFICATION the system by which all living things are organized.

CLIMATE CHANGE the process by which Earth's weather systems change over many years. Climate change is a natural process but human activity is increasing the speed of the changes.

COMMON ANCESTOR the species to which two or more living species are related. It is often extinct.

COMPOUND a substance that is made by combining one or more elements. Water is a compound, made of the two elements hydrogen and oxygen.

COMPUTER PROGRAM a set of instructions that a computer can follow to carry out a task.

CONDUCTOR a material that allows an electric current to flow through it easily. Metals are good conductors.

CURRENT ELECTRICITY a flow of electric charge that moves around a circuit of conductors.

D

DARK ENERGY a mysterious force that is making the universe expand faster and faster. It was only discovered about 20 years ago, and astronomers are still not sure what it is.

DNA (deoxyribonucleic acid) DNA typically exists as large molecules, found inside cells. It contains the information needed for a body to grow.

DNA PROFILING a way of spotting unique patterns in a person's DNA. It is often used in forensic science.

DOUBLE HELIX a helix is a three-dimensional spiral. A DNA molecule is a double helix, so it has two of these spirals wrapped around each other.

DWARF PLANET a body in orbit around the Sun that is big enough to have formed into a sphere, but is not big enough to have knocked everything else out of its orbit.

E

ECLIPSE an event where the Sun, Moon and Earth all line up for a short time. In a lunar eclipse, Earth sits in the middle and casts its shadow on the Moon. In a solar eclipse, the shadow of the Moon makes a strip of Earth's surface go dark as night for a few minutes.

ELECTRIC CHARGE a property of subatomic particles. Electrons have a negative charge while protons are positive. Neutrons are neutral and have no charge.

ELECTRIC GENERATOR a device that converts motion energy into electricity by spinning magnets at high speed.

ELECTRIC MOTOR a device that uses a magnetic field to make an electric wire move in a circle. Electric motors are used to power machines such as electric cars and computer hard drives.

ELECTRICITY the movement of electric charge so it moves as a current or gathers as a static charge on an object.

ELECTROMAGNETISM the field of science that studies electricity and magnetism, which are linked because one makes the other.

ELECTRON a subatomic particle with a negative charge. Atoms contain electrons.

ELEMENT a substance that cannot be separated into simpler ingredients. Every element is made of one type of atom. There are 90 natural elements, plus 28 synthetic ones. Examples of elements include carbon, gold and oxygen.

ENERGY the ability to do work or make a change to the system. There are several types of energy, including motion, sound and electricity.

ENGINEER someone who uses scientific knowledge to build something useful.

EVOLUTION the process by which new kinds of animals and plants develop from earlier kinds. It is usually a very slow process.

EXTINCTION when a species dies out.

F

FORCE a transfer of motion energy from one object to another, making it change the way it is moving.

FOSSIL remains of animals or plants that lived millions of years ago.

FOSSIL FUEL a carbon-rich fuel, such as coal, oil or natural gas, which formed millions of years ago from the remains of trees, microorganisms and other life forms.

FRICTION the force that happens when one moving object contacts another. The two surfaces drag on each other, making it harder to slide the objects past one another.

G

GALAXY a huge collection of stars, gas clouds, dust particles and other objects, such as planets and moons. There are billions of galaxies in the universe. Our solar system is part of the Milky Way Galaxy.

GENE a section of DNA that carries instructions for the manufacture of proteins for use by the cell. Proteins are very important chemicals used to build and run organisms.

GENOME the full collection of genes carried by the body's cells.

GEOCENTRIC THEORY the incorrect theory that Earth is at the centre of the universe, with the Sun, planets and stars going around it.

GLOBAL WARMING a process where the pollution produced by humans is changing the atmosphere in a way that is making Earth warm up. This is resulting in very big changes to the planet's weather systems.

GRAVITATIONAL WAVES ripples in space caused by the movement of matter. Heavy objects, such as black holes, make very powerful ripples that can be picked up by detectors on Earth.

GRAVITY the force that holds you to the ground and causes things to fall. It keeps the Moon moving around Earth, and Earth moving around the Sun.

GREENHOUSE EFFECT a natural process that warms Earth. Sunlight shines in from space and passes through the atmosphere, hitting the surface and making it warm. The heat radiates back into the air, but most of it is prevented from escaping into space by gases.

GREENHOUSE GAS a gas such as carbon dioxide or methane that traps heat as part of the greenhouse effect.

H

HELIOCENTRIC THEORY the incorrect theory that the Sun is the centre of the universe and the planets go around it. The Sun is indeed at the centre of the solar system but it is not the centre of the universe — there is no central point of the universe.

HYGIENE the practice of being clean to avoid becoming ill.

I

IMMUNITY an ability of the body to defend itself against a certain disease. Once the body has been infected it becomes immune to any future infections. Vaccines make people immune without having to have the illness first.

INDUSTRIAL REVOLUTION a period of major change in the way products were made. Beginning in England, workers moved from making handmade items in the home to large numbers of items in factories, using engine-powered machines.

INHERITANCE the process by which a person has received the genes from their mother and father and these genes provide the instructions to build their body.

INSULATOR a material that blocks an electric current. Plastics are excellent insulators.

K

KINETIC ENERGY the energy of motion.

KINGDOM the largest group of organisms in the classification system used to organize life, including the animal kingdom and plant kingdom.

L

LIGHT-YEAR the distance light travels in one year. One light-year is almost 10 trillion kilometres.

LUMINOSITY a measure of how bright an object is.

M

MACHINE LEARNING a system that allows a computer to learn how to do a job and program itself.

MAGNETIC FIELD the area around a magnet where its force acts, pulling and pushing on other objects.

MAGNETISM a force system that is most powerful in metals such as iron. Magnetic forces are able to push and pull on other objects.

MASS the amount of matter (stuff) an object contains. On Earth, an object's mass is the same as its weight. On the Moon, where the pull of gravity is lower, the object will weigh a lot less but its mass is exactly the same as on Earth.

MICROORGANISM a life form that is too small to see without a microscope.

MILKY WAY the galaxy in which Earth, the Sun and the other planets and objects in our solar system are found.

MOLECULE two or more atoms joined together.

N

NATURAL SELECTION process by which living things evolve over many generations. Individuals with features that make it easier for them to survive become more common, while individuals with weaker features die out.

NEUTRAL referring to an object that has no electric charge.

NEUTRON one of the subatomic particles that is found in the nucleus of an atom. Neutrons have no charge.

NOBEL PRIZE international prizes awarded every year to people who have achieved great things in science, or literature, or economics, or for world peace.

NUCLEUS (plural: nuclei) the core in the centre of something, such as a cell or atom.

O

ORBIT a repeated elliptical (oval) path that an object, such as a planet, takes around another object, such as the Sun.

ORGANISM a term that refers to any living thing, from the smallest bacterium to an oak tree or a blue whale.

P

PARTICLE any tiny lump of matter too small to see. Atoms are particles and so are electrons and protons.

PASTEURIZATION a way of preparing foods, such as milk, that removes most of the bacteria that will cause the food to go bad. The process involves heating the food to a very high temperature for a very short time.

PERIODIC TABLE a table of all known elements, ordered by increasing atomic number, and arranged in a way that reflects each element's atomic structure and chemical behaviours.

PESTICIDE a chemical poison that is sprayed on crops or in gardens to kill pests. The chemical is designed to affect only certain pests, but in general has many unwanted side-effects.

PHYSICS the study of the fundamental features of nature, such as matter, energy, light, heat, motion and electricity.

PROGRAMMING LANGUAGE a code used by computer programmers to set out clear instructions for a computer to follow. The finished code is then compiled, meaning it is converted into a string of binary numbers for the computer to use.

PROPERTIES what a substance is like and how it behaves. Physical properties relate to what we can see or measure, such as colour, texture and temperature. Chemical properties relate to how a substance behaves during a chemical reaction, such as how easily it burns.

PROTON a subatomic particle with a positive charge. Protons are located in the nuclei of atoms.

R

RADIATION a form of energy that moves as waves. Light, radio waves and microwaves are all types of radiation. Other radiation includes X-rays and gamma rays, which can have harmful effects on human bodies.

RADIATION POISONING the result of excessive exposure to radiation. It can lead to rapid death or diseases such as cancer.

RADIOACTIVITY when an atom's nucleus is too large and unstable to hold itself together and so it collapses, firing out subatomic particles and high-energy radiation. The most common radioactive elements on Earth are thorium and uranium.

REACTIVITY the likelihood of a substance to undergo a chemical reaction.

REDSHIFT a process that stretches the light waves that come from stars. Redshift tells us that a star or galaxy is moving away from us.

RELATIVITY a theory of how energy and mass change the shape of the space (and time) of the universe. This explains how gravity works.

RENEWABLE ENERGY a source of energy that will not run out, unlike energy released by burning fuels. Renewable energy includes solar power, wind, hydroelectricity and tide energy.

S

SEDNA a red, planet-like object in our solar system, discovered in 2003, which orbits the Sun and is situated beyond Pluto.

SOLAR POWER a power system that harnesses the energy in sunlight.

SOLAR SYSTEM the patch of space that is under the control of the Sun's gravity. It includes Earth and the Moon, along with the seven other planets, several dwarf planets and many thousands of smaller objects.

SPACETIME a way of understanding the universe that links time and space.

SPECIES a group of organisms that share so many features and characteristics that they are able to breed with each other and produce young that can themselves breed.

SPECTRUM the range of colours that is produced when light passes through a prism. A rainbow shows the colours in the spectrum.

SQUARED a mathematical idea where a number is multiplied by itself. For example, two squared is written as 2^2; the answer is 2 x 2 = 4.

STATIC ELECTRICITY when an electric charge is held on an object. The charge will not move until it has a path back to the ground (it is earthed). The static electricity then discharges as a spark. This could be a harmless electric shock.

STATISTICS a field of mathematics that collects a large number of measurements and arranges them in a way that allows you to understand more things about the subject being measured.

SUBATOMIC PARTICLE particles that are smaller than atoms, including electrons, protons and neutrons.

T

THERMODYNAMICS the science of heat energy.

TRAIT an inherited characteristic that is expressed in offspring, such as hair or eye colour. The trait is determined by the genes passed down from both parents. Inherited dominant genes are always expressed while an inherited recessive gene will only be expressed if paired with another recessive one.

TRANSFORMER an electric device that changes the voltage of an electric current. Transformers are used to control the voltages of our electricity supply.

TURING TEST a simple way of showing if a computer program has artificial intelligence. A human judge interviews two hidden contestants; one is a person, the other is the program. If the human judge cannot tell which is which then the computer is an AI. No program has ever passed the full test, which is named after Alan Turing, the computer scientist who thought it up.

U

UNIVERSAL FORCE the name given to the four forces that govern how all objects or particles interact. Gravity and electromagnetism are universal forces.

V

VACCINATION a medical technique for helping the body's immune system fight off deadly diseases. A medicine called a vaccine contains a less dangerous version of the disease. This teaches the immune system to recognize it so it can defend itself quickly if it becomes infected in future.

VIRUS a disease-causing agent. Catching a virus gives you diseases such as flu and chickenpox. The virus is a bundle of DNA and protein and cannot copy itself without the help of a living cell. This copying is what causes the diseases.

W

WIND POWER a way of turning the flow of air into electricity. This is normally done using a wind turbine, where the wind turns large rotor blades that spin an electricity generator.

WORK in science, work is anything where energy is used to change the motion of a piece of matter.

WORLD WIDE WEB a system that allows people to view the files stored on the many millions of computers connected by the internet without having to copy the files to their machine first.

X

X-RAY PHOTOGRAPHS a picture that is made using invisible X-rays instead of visible light. X-ray radiation has more energy in it than light so it can pass through solid objects, including the human body. Only the hard body parts, such as bone, block the X-rays, so an X-ray image shows up the bones inside the body, and is a useful way of looking for damage.